10

Excellent Reasons Not to Join the Military

10
Excellent Reasons Not to Join the Military

Edited by Elizabeth Weill-Greenberg

THE NEW PRESS

NEW YORK
LONDON

Requests for permission to reproduce selections from this book should
be mailed to: Permissions Department, The New Press, 38 Greene Street,
New York, NY 10013

Published in the United States by The New Press, New York, 2006
Distributed by W. W. Norton & Company, Inc., New York

Library of Congress Cataloging-in-Publication Data
10 Excellent reasons not to join the military / edited by
Elizabeth Weill-Greenberg.
p. cm.
ISBN-13: 978–1–59558–066–5 (pbk.)
ISBN-10: 1–59558–066–2 (pbk.)
1. United States—Armed Forces—Recruiting, enlistment, etc. 2. United
States—Armed Forces—Recruiting, enlistment, etc.—Iraq War, 2003—
3. Iraq War, 2003—Protest movements—United States. I. Title: Ten
excellent reasons not to join the military. II. Weill-Greenberg, Elizabeth.

UB323A615 2006
956.7044'3373—dc22   2005058230

The New Press was established in 1990 as a not-for-profit alternative to
the large, commercial publishing houses currently dominating the book
publishing industry. The New Press operates in the public interest rather
than for private gain and is committed to publishing, in innovative ways,
works of educational, cultural, and community value that are often
deemed insufficiently profitable.

www.thenewpress.com

Design and composition by Westchester Book Group
This book was set in Meta

Printed in the United States of America

2 4 6 8 10 9 7 5 3 1

Contents

Editor's Note

To keep the war in Iraq going, the military needs soldiers, lots and lots of them. So they have a multibillion-dollar advertising campaign. They sell adventure, money, education, camaraderie, purpose, and honor. The TV ads play relentlessly (often interrupting a vacuous episode of some dating show I'm enjoying on MTV). It's all variations on a theme: a young black kid tells his mom he found a way to pay for college; a man starts a new job and uses the skills he learned in the Army; a father tells his pudgy uniformed son he never shook his hand and looked him in the eye before. Fade to black . . . the U.S. Army.

What unfolds over the next one hundred pages or so are stories by military parents, soldiers, veterans, lawyers, and journalists about what doesn't make it into those ads. They discuss recruiters lying about college money, bonuses, and deployment. They describe the real life of a soldier—complete with lifelong injuries, inadequate care, insanity, and death.

This one little book may not be able to topple the machine it's up against. But the billions spent on advertising campaigns can't change one essential truth articulated in these chapters: the military is about war.

Acknowledgments

This book would not have been possible without Colin Robinson, who thought up the idea and gave me a chance. I will always be grateful for his sincerity, creativity, and support. Thank you to Elizabeth Seidlin-Bernstein for editorial input, careful editing of each line, and patiently answering my endless questions. I truly could not have completed this book without her tireless, immaculate work. Thank you to Charlotte Quinney, who meticulously fact-checked every chapter. Thank you to The New Press for believing in this project.

Thank you to each of the contributors for your courage, honest writing, and patience.

Thank you to every soldier, veteran, teacher, activist, parent, and student who believes there is honor in working for peace, not in killing. Thank you for bringing the soldiers of too many generations home. Without your work no war would ever end.

Thank you to my loving friends for their excitement, editorial suggestions, and collections of military ads: Eartha Melzer, Shane Smith, Tory Mack, and Sue and Daryl Strom.

Thank you to Dan Morris for believing in me, pushing me, and teaching me how to be generous without keeping score. And thank you to the memory of Peter Morris, who could make a cover letter sound like poetry.

Thank you to my family—Mom, Dad, Joanne, and Bummy—for making social justice part of my everyday life. I wish their professions—social workers, peace activists, and teachers—had the bloated budgets of the military.

Thank you to my boyfriend, Jon Whiten, who helped me through every step of this process in so many ways that even a Kelly Clarkson pop song couldn't capture them all.

10

Excellent Reasons Not to Join the Military

I'm fed up to the ears with old men dreaming up wars for young men to die in.

—George McGovern

When the rich wage war, it's the poor who die.

—Jean-Paul Sartre

Introduction
Cindy Sheehan

I always taught my four children from the time they were toddlers to use their words to solve conflicts.

I would tell them over and over that hitting, kicking, pinching, biting, scratching, hair pulling, and so forth were no way to solve problems. Starting when they were small, if my kids didn't know the right words to say to forestall violence, they would come to me and we would strategize about what to say and what to do, whether the conflicts were with siblings, classmates, teachers, or bosses.

Why can't countries learn to do this? Why, when the United States has a State Department devoted to diplomacy, are violence and killing so very often the first solution to problems real or imagined (as in the case of most wars)? Why, in a so-called civilized society, is the War Department—as the Department of Defense used to be called—the most highly funded and influential arm of our government?

Our family has always been very peaceful and nonviolent. The children rarely got spanked. We avoided all violence early in their lives. I firmly believe that one cannot teach peace by being violent. Imagine our family's surprise when our oldest child, Casey, came home and announced that he had enlisted in the Army. We were devastated.

Casey was in his third year of college when an Army recruiter lied to him, promising the sun and moon in order to get him to sign the enlistment contract. But the recruiter delivered none of his promises—only an early grave. We didn't know then that enlistment contracts are only binding on the recruit and not the government.

That is why this book is so important. What our family didn't know before Casey enlisted could fill a bookshelf. If we had known then what we know now, Casey never would have done what he thought was his duty as an American: to serve his country in a brave and noble way. We would have found other ways for him to serve his community.

In his seminal and very important work, *War is a Racket,* originally published in 1935, General Smedley D. Butler wrote: "War is a racket. It always has been. It is possibly the oldest, easily the most profitable, surely the most vicious. It is the only one international in scope. It is the only one in which the profits are reckoned in dollars and the losses in lives."

Casey was killed in action in Iraq on April 4, 2004. His recruiter had promised him that even if there were a war, Casey would never see combat. The one thing that our family didn't reckon on was that there would be a war. But, there had to be a war. War is inevitable in our society. Every decade or two, America has to be at war with someone.

Until the Vietnam conflict, we had always waged war against a clearly defined enemy with clearly defined leaders, uniforms, and boundaries. Until the Korean conflict, Congress had always declared war, as is their constitutional duty. Since then, not a single war has been formally declared by Congress.

In the 1950s, the war machine, with its vast opportunities for profits and power, chose the "Communists" to be our enemy and this led to our involvement in the Vietnam conflict. In the 1980s, Communism crumbled and the war machine needed a new enemy: terrorism.

The current invasion and occupation of Iraq is based on phony information. Our leaders are keeping our country terminally and falsely afraid of terrorism to foster its meddling in the Middle East.

We need to force our government to bring our troops home from Iraq now before the reckless and greedy leaders choose to invade Iran or Syria. We need to ensure that true peace and diplomacy are used in the future, and that we look back in history on immoral and illegal wars as horrors of an inhumane era.

We the people, especially the moms, of America need to wake up and realize that wars are seldom fought to preserve our freedom and democracy, but rather to make rich people richer and powerful people even more powerful.

We need to stop allowing the war machine to eat our children and spit out money.

We need to realize that violence and killing are rarely, if ever, solutions to any problems. We need to demand that our leaders use their words to solve problems. We need to demand that other nations use their words, too.

We need to wake up and realize that our world is growing smaller every day, that we are all part of the human race, and that we don't have to run it to win.

We need to run to our humanity and away from war.

Let this book be the beginning of the end of the military industrial complex. Our very survival on this planet demands it.

Enjoy the book and pass it on to all your friends.

Peace now,
Cindy Sheehan
Co-founder of Gold Star Families for Peace
Mother of four amazing children

WHAT HAPPENS DURING DEPLOYMENT?

Deployment is when an Active Duty or Army Reserve unit is sent to a specific area of operations, usually on foreign soil—most recently in Afghanistan, Kuwait, and Iraq. Yet a common misperception is that a deployed unit is automatically sent to a war zone. Oftentimes, units are deployed to non-combat regions, including Hawaii, Italy, Germany, and South Korea. Or they are utilized for humanitarian efforts, such as helping civilians rebuild their lives after a natural disaster. . . .

—From the "For Parents" section of the Go Army Web site, http://www.goarmy.com/ for_parents/deployment.jsp

1

You may be killed
Cindy Sheehan

Cindy Sheehan's son, Casey, was killed in Iraq on April 4, 2004. Since his death Cindy has traveled the country speaking out against the war and the Bush administration. She co-founded Gold Star Families for Peace, an organization of antiwar military family members whose loved ones were killed in Iraq.

In August 2005 she gained international attention when she set up Camp Casey outside George Bush's ranch in Crawford, Texas, and demanded to meet with him and know "for what noble cause" her son was murdered. At the time of this writing, she is still waiting for an answer.

"You're looking at the newest recruit in the U.S. Army," Casey proudly announced to his dad and me on that warm May evening in the year 2000.

His dad and I were devastated. We had no idea he was going down to the MEPS (Military Entrance Processing Station) to enlist that day. He was gone for hours and hours. I tried to call him on his cell phone all day, but I got no response.

Seeing that I was so upset by his news that he thought was good, Casey tried to reassure me by saying: "Don't worry mom, Sergeant 'So and So' told me to tell you not to worry. He said that I scored so high on the ASVAB [Armed Services Vocational Aptitude Battery, the military assessment test] that even if there was a war, I would never see combat. I will only be going in a support role."

Well, long story short, Casey, a Humvee mechanic, was killed in combat five days after he arrived in Iraq.

Casey, my oldest child, was born on May 29, 1979, after a long labor. It was Memorial Day that year and John F. Kennedy's birthday. I could tell right from the beginning that Casey Austin Sheehan

Army recruitment ad

was going to be a great man. He would look at me with those dark, piercing eyes and it seemed like he could see right through me and that little tiny baby boy knew exactly what I was thinking.

Casey was the best baby in recorded history. He rarely cried, so if and when he ever did, I knew that something was terribly wrong with him. As a matter of fact, after he was six months old and he went to his own room in a big crib, he would wake up every morning and start to play with his crib gym. We would hear the rattles and beeps of the gym and the cooing and laughing of Casey every morning. Casey's morning play would give his dad and me a few extra moments of sleep.

From the minute Casey was born though, I promised him as I nursed him that I would never, ever let him go off to war. I rarely break my promises and I will never forgive myself for breaking such an important one to my big boy.

Casey was a normal kid who loved his life, music, animals, and playing—whether it was baseball, wrestling, or video games. He loved playing with his younger siblings (Carly, Andy, and Janey) and his action figures. Until he was about eight years old, every night that his dad and I tucked him in, he would say: "Thanks, mom and dad. This was the best day of my life!" What a cheerful and loving thing to say every night! How can a mom go wrong with a son like that?

Casey, like most kids, didn't like cleaning his room or doing his homework. But he rarely, if ever, talked back to us or fought with his sisters and brother. He never got in trouble at school and was often awarded good conduct awards and named "Student of the Month."

When Casey grew up, he still loved baseball, wrestling, playing video games, hanging out with his siblings, music, animals, and his life. He was an altar server at church for ten years. Casey was a theater arts major in college, and one of the things we loved to do together was go to the movies. The last movie we saw together was *Peter Pan,* during his Christmas leave in 2003. Little did I know he would be dead in less than three months. Every time I fly now, I look out at the clouds and remember that movie and try to see Casey.

The day Casey went in the Army was the saddest day of my life up until then. We took him out to dinner and an IMAX movie. Then we dropped him off at the hotel, where he would leave for boot camp the next day. I sobbed all the way home. He was, after all, my firstborn and my first to fly from the nest.

Casey had a tough time in boot camp. He wasn't in good physical condition and he missed being home. I would send him lots of cards and mail. I was a Catholic youth minister, and every Sunday my youth group wrote him cards and letters too. I tried to encourage him as much as possible. I wish I had told him to fail, but I didn't know he could do that and get out of the military. Graduating from boot camp was something that Casey wanted to do, so we supported him as much as possible.

One phone call from boot camp was troubling only in hindsight. Casey called and told me that he had made me the beneficiary of his life insurance. I laughed and said that wouldn't be necessary and when he got married, he could change his policy to make his wife his beneficiary.

Casey finally did graduate from boot camp and was sent to the First Cavalry Division at Fort Hood, Texas. He settled into his life as a Humvee mechanic, even though he really wanted to be a chaplain's assistant as promised by his recruiter. We missed each other but we got to visit at least once a year, and we talked on the phone just about every day.

Casey was killed in Iraq on April 4, 2004. That day, at about 6 P.M. Iraqi time, his division had just taken over command of Forward Operating Base War Eagle in Sadr City from the First Armored Division. Fifty-three minutes later, Casey was killed in an ambush by Shi'a militants loyal to Moqtada al Sadr. Like I said before, Casey had been in Baghdad for only five days.

Casey was killed at 7:53 A.M. California time. It was a Sunday, Palm Sunday. I didn't even get out of bed until 9:00 A.M. Little did I know that my precious boy was already dead when I got up to go to breakfast with my best friend. Little did I know that my life was about to be devastated on a scale too terrible for anyone to imagine.

I went through the entire day, worried about Casey, but otherwise normally until about 5:00 P.M. Casey's dad, Pat, and I were eating dinner in the living room and watching CNN. A burning

Humvee was being shown and we heard that eight soldiers were killed in Baghdad that day. I instantly knew that one of the soldiers was Casey. I told my husband. He started screaming at me that I needed help if I was going to freak out every time I watched the news. Pat's yelling was to no avail, though, as I was sure that one of the dead was Casey.

At about 8:30 P.M. we still hadn't heard that Casey was KIA, so I took our little dogs, Buster and Chewy, for their evening walk. All the way around our route though, I was crying. I knew Casey was dead, or very injured at least. When I came around the corner of the garage with the dogs, heading for the house, I saw my worst nightmare: three Army officers standing in my living room. I immediately knew why they were there.

I lunged in the house and dropped the dogs' leashes. Pat was standing up holding the pair of pants he was folding, and our oldest daughter, Carly, was standing in the doorway in shock. She had just gotten home from work a few seconds before.

I collapsed on the floor screaming: "No! No! No! Not Casey! Please God, no!"

I don't know how long I screamed. But I am sure my screaming that night shortened my life by a good measure. Hearing that a child is killed is so violent and horrible. That moment was the closest I have ever come to dying without actually doing so. In fact, I prayed for the Angel of Death to stretch his ugly hand over me and take me that night. He didn't. He is not merciful.

Thus began my life of heartache. Thus began my long, awful days of pain and despair and my dark, ugly nights of pain and despair.

We buried my cherished child on April 13, 2004. He posthumously received medals and full military honors. I received my "Gold Star" after joining the dubious ranks of the Gold Star Mothers on April 4, 2004. A Gold Star Mother who had two sons killed in Vietnam pinned my Gold Star on me at Casey's funeral like it was some demented Girl Scout Badge that I should be proud of.

Since Casey's death, I have set out on a quest to bring the lies that killed him into the light of day.

I have worked to try to tell this country how painful it is to lose a child to lies. I have tried to prevent what happened to Casey and me from happening to anyone else.

The lies and Casey's murder have cost my family so much: our Casey, happy days in the future. Our lives have been torn apart, and it ultimately cost us our idea of being a family. My obsession with bringing out the truth has cost me my marriage of twenty-eight years to Pat.

The Sheehan family will never be able to have another holiday or family celebration without that empty hole in our hearts and souls that Casey being killed in a war has created. We will know, always, that we are incomplete when we are all together again. It sucks, and the devastation of Casey's death is so unnecessary and cruel.

Casey's death has led to the Camp Casey movement that began when I sat down in Crawford, Texas, in August 2005 and refused to move until George W. Bush spoke to me and told me for what noble cause Casey and the others have died. Camp Casey has spurred an entire peace movement, and we have Casey's life to thank for that.

I told you earlier that I knew Casey was going to be a great man. I just never realized how great, or how much agony his moment of greatness would cause me.

Don't join the military. The recruiters lie. They never tell you that you may die and put your mom in hell. Don't do it. It's not worth it.

A soldier who is able to see the humanity of the enemy makes a troubled and ineffective killer.

—Chris Hedges, *War Is a Force That Gives Us Meaning*

2

You may kill others who do not deserve to die
Paul Rockwell

Paul Rockwell, formerly assistant professor of philosophy at Midwestern State University in Texas, is a writer in the Bay Area and a columnist for In Motion Magazine *and* Common Dreams.

When Marine Sergeant Jimmy Massey enlisted in the Marines, he never expected that he would be ordered to kill civilians. He enlisted in good faith, and he trusted his commander in chief to tell the truth, to follow the Geneva Conventions and the rule of law. He was even ready to risk his life for his country in the event that the United States faced a real or imminent attack.

In January 2003, Jimmy was deployed to Iraq. During the initial invasion he says he was involved in a number of "checkpoint killings," the kind of atrocities that occur over and over today without fanfare or scandal.

A hard-core Marine, Jimmy was in charge of a platoon of machine gunners and missile men. It was their job to secure the road out of Baghdad. As bombs rained down on the ancient city of five million people, civilians fled in panic. There was chaos at the checkpoints.

"All Iraqis," Jimmy told me in a recent interview, "were considered a menace."

"One particular incident really pushed me over the edge. It involved a car with Iraqi civilians. We fired some warning shots, but the car did not slow down. So we lit 'em up. Well, this particular vehicle we didn't destroy completely, and one gentleman on the ground looked up at me and said, 'Why did you kill my brother? We didn't do anything wrong.' That hit me like a ton of bricks."

Jimmy was involved in four more checkpoint tragedies. He was also ordered to shoot into a youthful crowd on the outskirts of Baghdad, near a military compound. "There were demonstrators

Army recruitment ad

at the end of the street. They were young and they had no weapons."

It was the higher command that gave the order to wipe out the demonstrators. "We used M-16s and .50-caliber machine guns," Jimmy said. "Six to ten kids were taken out."

Like thousands of his fellow Marines and soldiers, who also enlisted in good faith, Jimmy was trapped—trapped between atrocity and near-sedition. If he followed orders, he might commit war crimes. If he disobeyed orders, he put his own life and career in jeopardy.

Marines are trained to kill without remorse. But there are times in life when indoctrination, reprisals, and threats of humiliation fail to erase that inner feeling that we are all God's children. A Marine who recognizes the humanity of the people whose country is under occupation makes an ineffective killer. Repelled by the indiscriminate carnage and the visible suffering of the Iraqi people, who only deserved to be left alone by outside powers, Jimmy repudiated the war. He refused to participate in apparent war crimes. He defied authority, and his commander called him a coward and put him under a "kind of house arrest." Jimmy, a real fighter, eventually won his honorable discharge.

At his home in North Carolina, Jimmy says the U.S. military is committing war crimes. "Yes, I killed innocent people for my government. And for what? I feel like I've had a hand in some sort of evil lie at the hands of our government. I just feel embarrassed, ashamed about it. . . . I spend long hours speechless and looking at the wall, seeing nothing but images of dead Iraqis."

Like Jimmy Massey, Darrell Anderson is fighting the dark ghosts of atrocity. A twenty-two-year-old GI from Lexington, Kentucky, who won a Purple Heart after he was wounded, Anderson was stationed at a checkpoint near a police station in Baghdad when a speeding car swerved in his direction. Darrell said he received orders to shoot. There was a family in the car—two children, a man, and his wife. Darrell's buddies screamed; "Shoot! Why don't you shoot? Why don't you shoot?"

He simply could not pull the trigger of his M-16. "The car posed no threat," he told me.

"My superior came over and said, 'What are you

doing?' I said, 'Look, there's children in the back. It's a family. I did the right thing. It's wrong to fire in this situation.' My superior told me: 'No, you did the wrong thing. You will fire next time, or you will be punished. That's our orders.'"

American soldiers are under constant pressure to kill Iraqi civilians, Darrell said. "At traffic stops, we kill innocent people all the time. If you are fired on from the street, you are supposed to fire on everybody that is there. If I am in a market, I shoot people who are buying groceries."

The indiscriminate use of artillery is a direct violation of the Geneva Conventions, which state (Part IV, Article 48) that combatants "shall at all times distinguish between the civilian population and combatants and between civilian objects and military objectives and, accordingly, shall direct their operations only against military objectives."

Darrell Anderson said he was riding in his self-propelled Howitzer when he was ordered to fire rounds into downtown Najaf in response to a mortar attack. Artillery rounds are filled with little BBs or shrapnel. Like cluster bombs, the "kill-ratio" is wide, and bystanders are covered in the blanket of destruction. Under orders, Darrell said, "we fired about seventy or eighty rounds. My buddies came back and said, 'We killed a lot of people.' About 100 civilians. They were just people downtown. Killing downtown civilians is a typical incident."

I remember watching old World War II films where Nazis in Poland or Czechoslovakia would call civilians into the street, line them up, and threaten reprisals if they did not yield vital information. Occupiers need intelligence, but local natives rarely give information voluntarily. From the U.S. raids on hamlets in Vietnam, to the French raids in the Casbah in Algeria, to the ongoing door-to-door raids in Iraq, the main features of imperial occupations have never changed.

Darrell was involved in numerous nighttime raids on Iraqi homes. "When we raid homes in the middle of the night," Darrell explains, "twenty guys blow through the house at gunpoint, and it's pretty terrifying for all the Iraqi families. We kick down the doors or bash them with a sledgehammer. One team goes in to clear the bottom floor. The second team heads upstairs. The women are screaming and crying, the children are freakin' out, and the men ask us, 'Why, why, what have we done?' We separate the women, and their men are handcuffed and taken away. Even if we are looking for a single person, all the men are considered enemy until proven otherwise.

"Once we raided a home based on faulty information we got from a drunk. We paid him for the tip. We busted into a house and yanked some guy out and sent him to Abu Ghraib for torture. . . . Sometimes we closed off the whole section of a city and raided a couple hundred homes, door-to-door."

Darrell described the almost ceaseless brutality of the occupation. "In downtown Baghdad, there were three guys going to their car. One Iraqi opened the door and reached inside. The guys in our Humvee—a machine-gunner and an NCO in charge—fired on the Iraqis. Our gunners said the Iraqis could have been going for weapons. So we just killed them. There were no weapons in the vehicle. Three innocent guys, and there was no investigation."

Darrell compares Iraq to the tragedy of Vietnam,

another American war in which unseen, distant commanders, whose own lives were never in danger, sent vulnerable young men and women into situations where war crimes become an everyday aspect of military conduct. "Baghdad is in rubble," he said. "The big buildings were blown up. Many were targets, and houses in Najaf are blown to pieces."

Today Darrell is a war resister. He left the military and escaped to Canada, where he is seeking political asylum. "I can't go back to the war. If I return to Iraq, I have no choice but to commit atrocities. And I don't want to kill innocent people."

Aidan Delgado, an Army Reservist in the 320th Military Police Company, witnessed horrific atrocities in Iraq. He served as a mechanic from April 2003 to April 2004, and he was stationed at Abu Ghraib for six months.

I first met Aidan at a high school in northern California, where he presented graphic images of the U.S. occupation. "If you're old enough to go to war," Aidan said to the seniors, "you're old enough to know what goes on. I want to let you know what you are signing on for if you enlist."

"It was common practice," his narrative began, "to set up blockades. The Third Infantry would block off a road. In advance of the assaults, civilians would flee the city in panic. As they approached us, someone would yell: 'Stop, stop!' in English. Of course many couldn't understand. Their cars were blown up with cannons, or crushed with tanks. Killing non-combatants happened routinely, not only with the Third Infantry, but the First Marines."

Aidan's experiences at Abu Ghraib turned him against the entire war. His duties at the prison led him to discover that most of the prisoners had never been insurgents. (According to the May 2004 Taguba report on Iraqi prisoner abuse at Abu Ghraib, many of the detainees never committed acts against U.S. forces.)

The living conditions at the prison were inhumane. Behind barbed wire, the prisoners launched a protest that got rough. Rocks were thrown. "The guards asked permission to use lethal force, and they got it," Aidan said. "They opened fire on the prisoners with the machine guns. They shot twelve and killed three. I talked to one guy who did the killing. He showed me grisly photographs and bragged about the results. 'Look, I shot this guy in the face,' he said. 'See, his head is split open.' He talked like the Terminator. I was stunned and said, 'You shot an unarmed man behind barbed wire for throwing a stone.' He said to me, 'Well, I said a prayer, and I gunned him down.' There was a complete disconnect between what he had done and his morality. He was the nicest guy, a family man, a courteous, devout Christian."

When Aidan finished his high school presentation, I saw a student who looked almost ill in the back row. I later learned that, a day earlier, he had enlisted in the Army.

Aidan challenged the students to confront the issue of atrocity, to overcome denial, to consider the military, not as a career or an opportunity, but as a way of life that claims and smothers souls.

The reality of torture and other war crimes presents a moral challenge to all young men and women considering a career in military service.

Under the impact of Aidan's testimony, the high school students began to wonder: "Will I be ordered to commit atrocities or war crimes, to carry out policies against my own religion and conscience, deeds that I may regret for the rest of my life?"

Moved by Aidan's narrative, I began to reflect on past abuses in American military history. I recall the anguish of Paul Meadlo's mother when she discovered that her son committed atrocities at My Lai: "I gave them a good boy, and they sent me back a murderer." And she wanted to know: What did the military do to her son?[1]

War crimes in Iraq are not mere aberrations. They emanate from official policies regarding the aims and conduct of the occupation.

It is official policy, for example, to use cluster bombs in populated areas. Soldiers and Marines merely carry out the policy.

It was official policy, under Operation Iron Ham-

---

1. Seymour Hersh, speaking at the University of Illinois Conference "Can Freedom of the Press Survive Media Consolidation?" May 10, 2005.

mer, to put barbed wire around villages, to bull-doze crops, to bomb homes, and to hold families in jail until they released insurgent information.[2] In his attempt to justify the punitive expedition, it was reported that Captain Todd Brown, company commander of the 4th Infantry Division, stated, "You have to understand the Arab mind. . . . The only thing they understand is force—force, pride and saving face."[3]

It was official policy to level Fallujah, a city of 300,000 people, as an act of collective punishment. American commanders openly declared that Fallujah needed to be taught a lesson. Commanders ordered the use of 500-pound bombs that are utterly indiscriminate in their effects. No type of building—mosques, homes, medical facilities—was exempt from aerial destruction. At a mass burial of dead Iraqis, Marine Captain P.J. Batty stated: "Everyone needs to understand

2. Cockburn, Patrick. "U.S. Troops Bulldoze Crops." *Counterpunch,* October 14, 2003.

3. Wilkins, Dexter. "Tough New Tactics by U.S. Tighten Grip on Iraq Towns." *New York Times,* December 7, 2003.

there are consequences for not following the Iraqi government."[4]

In her recent book, *One Woman's Army,* former commanding general of Abu Ghraib Janis Karpinski exposes the connections between the use of torture at Guantánamo, in Afghanistan, and in cell blocks 1A and 1B at Abu Ghraib. Major General Geoffrey Miller, Attorney General Alberto Gonzales, and Secretary of Defense Donald Rumsfeld played key roles in the preparation and execution of torture policy.

Although Karpinski does not excuse the acts of reservists at Abu Ghraib, she reminds us that those who actually authorized the use of dogs, hooding, sleep deprivation, stress positions, and isolation—techniques of torture—avoid accountability for the consequences of their own decisions. During the Abu Ghraib scandal, neither Rumsfeld, Miller, nor Gonzales—not one top official

---

4. Harris, Edward. "Iraqis Remove Fallujah's Corpses under U.S. Marine Plan Honoring Islamic Death Rites." Associated Press, November 16, 2004.

or commander—stepped forward to share responsibility with the reservists. In essence, Karpinski makes clear, American commanders left their soldiers in the lurch.

Every American youth who considers military enlistment needs to take a close look at military "justice." Not only are American Marines, reservists, and soldiers expected to follow unlawful orders, but they are also expected to bear lifelong burdens of shame, guilt, and legal culpability for the arrogance of their own commanders—who dispense life and death from an office computer. Even before the invasion of Iraq in April 2003, more than 600 U.S. veterans signed a "Call to Conscience," expressing remorse for past war crimes. They wrote, "In the last Gulf War, as troops, we were ordered to murder from a safe distance. We remember the road to Basra—the Highway of Death—where we were ordered to kill fleeing Iraqis. We bulldozed trenches, burying people alive."[5]

Once a student makes that fateful decision to enlist in the U.S. military today—once an individual,

---

5. www.calltoconscience.net.

through basic training, is conditioned to kill without remorse, to become an occupier in a country where insurgents are indistinguishable from neighbors, friends, and family in their own homeland—it is too late to turn back. As warhistorian Gwynne Dyer writes: "Men will kill under compulsion—men will do almost anything if they know it is expected of them and they are under strong social pressure to comply."[6]

"Only exceptional people can resist atrocity—producing situations," writes psychiatrist Robert Jay Lifton in *Superpower Syndrome*.[7] Jimmy Massey, Darrell Anderson, Aidan Delgado, and scores of other war resisters are exceptional men and women. When they enlisted, they only wanted to serve their country. They hoped to make a difference. But the military transported them beyond the rule of law, turning them into occupiers of Iraq, not defenders of democracy. These war

6. Grossman, Dave. *On Killing*. New York: Back Bay, 1995, p. 30.

7. Lifton, Robert Jay. *Superpower Syndrome: America's Apocalyptic Confrontation with the World*. Nation Books, October 2003 .

resisters fought back and broke the military code of silence.

Americans can hold on to their humanity, to be sure. But only by recognizing the humanity, not only of Arab peoples, but of all peoples who have a right to self-determination.

Refusing to enlist is more than a career decision. It is a moral and political act, a contribution to the burgeoning, international movement for a better, more peaceful world. It is an affirmation of the sacredness of life and the dignity of all humanity.

A great war leaves the country with three armies—an army of cripples, an army of mourners, and an army of thieves.

—German proverb

In war, there are no unwounded soldiers.

—José Narosky

3

You may be injured
Robert Acosta and Nina Berman

Robert Acosta lost his hand and sustained other serious injuries while serving in Iraq. Since returning he has traveled the country, speaking out against the war.

Nina Berman is a documentary photographer and author of the book Purple Hearts: Back from Iraq, *a series of portraits and interviews with American soldiers who were wounded in Iraq, including Robert. In 2005, she received a World Press Award and a grant from the Open Society Institute in honor of this work. She resides in New York City, where she also teaches at the International Center of Photography.*

Robert:

I grew up in Santa Ana, California. A tough place to grow up. By the age of seventeen, I was working at a local movie theater, using drugs, and had long dropped out of school completely. My best friend had just returned from basic training and introduced me to his recruiter. After a few months of meeting with the Army staff sergeant, I finally agreed to take my G.E.D. test, the equivalent to a high school diploma and a requirement for joining the Army. By August 2001, I was on my way to Fort Leonard Wood, Missouri, for basic combat training. About a month later, the Twin Towers were attacked. I remember that day like it was yesterday. Our commander came in front of the company and said that both towers had been hit, and that it was an attack but the attackers were unknown. The first thought that ran through my mind, and I'm sure many others, was we are going to war! But I can't say I was scared; it was more of a shock. Of course we knew nothing but what they told us because we weren't allowed to watch television.

The buildup to the war started in late 2002, or at least that's when I started paying attention to it.

Robert Acosta © Nina Berman

I remember being home on leave, my mom asking me questions like, "Are you going?" or "Will I be able to talk to you?" But I always shrugged it off as no big deal: "Don't worry mom, everything will be fine!" After returning from leave to Germany, where I was stationed with the 1st Armored Division, we started hearing rumors about deploying to Iraq. I remember walking to work early in the morning and seeing the *Stars and Stripes* front page headline: "1st AD receives orders to deploy!" Soon after, our commander stood before us and read the orders for us to deploy. The night we left was all chaos. It was really hard seeing families split up. Then we arrived in Kuwait.

I got to call home almost every other day, which would change once we moved north. We stayed in a place called Camp Udairi, not too far from the Kuwait-Iraq border. The whole 1st Armored Division was there, and little by little troops were moving north. We heard stories of soldiers still getting ambushed and little kids stabbing them through the thin plastic on Humvee doors. After about a week or two, we got word we were moving up.

We traveled for two and a half days through a

combination of empty highways, dirt roads, and open desert. We only stopped when we fueled up and ate on the road. We passed through a few villages where people were really friendly, and other places where you knew not to stay long. But we made it to Baghdad safely.

I was an ammunition specialist, so my job mainly consisted of supplying and storing all types of ammunition. I remember an incident that seriously still makes me think a lot. Sitting at the AHA (ammunition holding area) one morning with one of my buddies, we heard two loud thumps off in the distance. A split second later a 40mm grenade flew right by his head, bounced off a water can ten feet away, and landed between us. But it didn't go off. If it had, we would have been done! That was the first time I got to call home. But of course I told my parents everything was cool. I just wanted to hear their voices.

There were other incidents here and there, but nothing too crazy. Sometimes we went out and talked to the locals, who seemed harmless. On many afternoons, a friend and I would go to purchase ice and sodas from the people who set up tents along the road. On one of those trips we went all the way to the end of the road, and both of us started to feel nervous. All of a sudden hostile Iraqis appeared and they tossed a hand grenade into my vehicle. My first reaction was to grab it, so I did, but I accidentally dropped it on the floor between my feet. I reached for it again, then Boom!

The next thing I knew, the smoke had cleared and I was awake. I looked down to see my hand gone and my legs mangled. I can remember every detail from that moment on because I stayed awake until the doctor put me out about twenty minutes later. I looked down after the smoke cleared: my hand had been completely mutilated and both my legs were broken. My buddy was OK, and he saved my life. The road back was packed with cars and people. The only way to get back was to plow through everything in our path. Our vehicle died once it reached the front gate and my buddy carried me on his back to another vehicle. But even today he has problems like myself—it's not easy to come home and try to fit in after the things we saw that day.

After seven long, hard months of surgeries, physical therapy, occupational therapy, and the slow realization that I lost my hand, I finally got to go home. But it only got harder. Upon coming home, I not only had trouble with the VA, but also people just didn't know what was happening. One time this man actually asked me, "Is the war still going on?"

Looking back, I realize that coming home was the hardest part. I still have pain in my legs; my left hand gets sore due to overuse; I can't sleep at night; and I get spooked really easily. Since I've been home, every night has been such a struggle to fall asleep.

I left for the military thinking I was going into a better life where I could travel and not deal with all the negativity of home. Now I'm stuck here in Santa Ana and I can't work. I even tried school but that got really stressful. I wasn't sleeping enough. And people constantly asking me questions like "Was it hot?" or "Did you shoot anyone?" really took its toll.

I try not to think about it, but my hand is a constant reminder. The point I'm trying to make is that there are other options out there. The military doesn't care about you—you're just a number, a chess piece.

Nina:

I first met Robert Acosta at the Walter Reed Army Medical Center in Washington, D.C., in October of 2003. I was at the hospital photographing amputees for a magazine article when I wandered into a back room and saw Robert sitting at a small table watching a man paint little black lines, meant to look like hair, on what would be Robert's new right arm.

It turned out Robert didn't like wearing that fake arm, it kept breaking and ripping, so he got rid of it and just goes with his hook or lets his stump hang free. Since returning home, he's tattooed his chest and arms. One image shows an exploding grenade. When I asked him why all the body art, he replied that he hopes when people stare at him, rather than being repelled by his amputation, they will admire the artwork.

Robert is one of twenty severely wounded soldiers I photographed for a book called *Purple Hearts: Back from Iraq*. The book contains just a small sample of the tens of thousands of soldiers and Marines who have returned home wounded and permanently disabled. According to the

Department of Defense, as of this writing 15,704 men and women were wounded in combat. They have lost pieces of their brain, eyes, ears, organs, and limbs. Some will be in wheelchairs for the rest of their lives. Others are so severely burned that doctors are using the skin of pigs to patch their faces. But that isn't even the whole story. Many more thousands of young men and women have been injured in combat support, and they aren't even counted by the Department of Defense.

Take, for example, the story of a soldier named Luis, a quadriplegic at twenty-two years old. He is confined to a wheelchair. He can't feel anything from the chest down. This young man, who left a small town in Puerto Rico to join the Army, was riding in a tank near Tikrit on May 5, 2003, when his commander told him to destroy a concrete wall that had a mural of Saddam Hussein on it. Luis followed the order but chunks of concrete came tumbling into the tank's hatch, severing his spinal cord. Luis spent seven months, first at Walter Reed and then at the Miami Veterans hospital, before the Army medically discharged him. During that time he couldn't collect veterans benefits, which he desperately needed, even though his dad, a career military man, was advocating night and day for his son's rights.

When I met Luis, he could hardly speak. His young wife, her teeth still in braces, was feeding him on his hospital bed. They were trying to have a positive outlook, but it was more than either of them could fathom. And yet in all of this, Luis wasn't even counted in the Department of Defense tally of the wounded.

Of course not every soldier returns a quadriplegic. The first two soldiers I photographed were blind. One was in the war for only a few weeks when a piece of metal from an artillery shell pierced his brain. His head is held together with titanium plates. He's brain damaged, prone to seizures, and has personality disorders. This strong young man, a college graduate, handsome, with a bright future, now needs his parents to take him to the bathroom.

He'll tell you everything is OK. He says he has no regrets. He had some fun over there. He was proud to serve his country. What else is he supposed to say? At least he has support from his family. Not all soldiers are so lucky.

Many of the young men I photographed joined the Army to get away from miserable homes, dead-end towns, gangs, drugs, or just boredom. They went to Iraq to escape violence and depression, and now they are back where they started, in the same old towns, with the same problems, except now it's worse. They don't have their bodies, they don't have their strength, and many, suffering from post-traumatic stress disorder (PTSD), have lost their minds.

I met one soldier who was living alone in a trailer, completely blind, without a leg, shrapnel wounds covering his body. He has no parents to take care of him and spends his days with young kids who ride around in circles on ATVs on a dead-end road in one of the poorest counties in his state. On the anniversary of his injury, he was found wandering at night through the woods in what local news reports said was an apparent suicide attempt. Do you think the Army recruiting commercial that seduced this soldier into joining ever mentioned anything about blindness, amputation, or brain damage?

One might be tempted to say, "Well, I'm going to

Iraq as a truck driver, or an ammo guy; it's not like I'm in the 82nd Airborne or in the Marines. I'll be safe." But no one is safe. Everywhere is a combat zone. Most of the soldiers I photographed were doing the most mundane things when their arms and legs were blown off. One was delivering ice. Robert was getting something to eat. Another was stuck in traffic. Another was standing guard at a bank. Out of nowhere came a rocket-propelled grenade, a suicide bomber, or a roadside bomb. In one second, your life will never be the same and no matter how smart or how good of a soldier you may be, there is little you can do to protect yourself or your friends from a powerful insurgency that wears no uniform, has no clear battle lines, and strikes at will.

Being concerned about your health and well-being does not make a person a coward. If you are not concerned, no one else is going to be. The people who preach that giving life or limb for country is the highest honor are the very same people who didn't provide armor for Humvees and voted to give tax breaks for rich people instead of money for veterans benefits. Wounded soldiers from the Iraq war are being turned away from veterans hospitals or put on waiting lists that can stretch for months (as addressed in the next chapter). Keep this in mind when the Army recruiter pushes pamphlets at you and tells you how exciting the Army is. Then ask him how much money he makes for signing you up.

I am not a veteran and it is not for me to say whether a young man or woman should join the military at this moment in time. That is your choice. But if you are thinking about joining, please take a minute and consider this: your decision may have irreversible consequences of the most painful and personal nature, affecting your body, mind, and soul for the rest of your life. Then ask yourself a more obvious question. Why is it that the politicians who are urging you to enlist, who are offering you huge signing bonuses and selling you dreams of heroism and glory, aren't suiting up their own kids and sending them off to get blown to bits in Iraq?

After a war, a hero is just a man with one leg.

—Anonymous

4

You may not receive proper medical care

Adele Kubein

Adele Kubein was active in the peace movement during the Vietnam era. After 9/11, Adele began to write op-ed columns for the local papers regarding the need for foreign policy reform. In 1998 her daughter signed up with the National Guard. In November 2002, Adele joined Military Families Speak Out. She has traveled around the United States and to Japan as an MFSO spokesperson, giving dozens of speeches and press conferences over the last three years.

Adele's daughter has requested that her name not be used publicly because she is still an active-duty soldier, dependent on the Army to provide her with wages and medical care. She has been asked by her superiors to remain silent and warned that her name should no longer be used by her mother in public.

Suck it up! That is what my daughter, a National Guard soldier, was told as she limped around using a cane bought from an Iraqi street vendor.

When her helicopter was shot down she knew her leg was hurt, but convoys need people who can repair trucks and shoot their way out of ambushes, so her superiors ignored the limp. She did not insist on treatment because she was cowed into keeping her pain to herself.

By November, she was manning a .50-caliber gun mounted on a Humvee on convoys for two months with a broken leg, which had not been treated. This was not as worrisome as the fact that no body armor to fit her had been found. A broken leg is minor when people are aiming at your chest. Of course, there is the problem of not being able to run from a burning vehicle; but so far, so good.

Finally an officer from another unit spotted my daughter limping and ordered her to the field hospital for X rays, where the shattered bone in her

SERVE AROUND THE WORLD — OR AROUND THE CORNER.

As a Soldier in **AN ARMY OF ONE**, you could be assigned to an overseas duty station such as Hawaii, Alaska, the Far East, Europe and more. You can even pick your first duty station if available. As an Army Reserve Soldier, you'll be assigned to a Reserve unit close to where you live or attend school. No matter which option you choose, you'll be maximizing your potential and gaining valuable experience. Further, you'll be working with young men and women from all walks of life, with goals and ambitions much like your own. Together you'll experience a unique and rewarding way of life — as Soldiers in **AN ARMY OF ONE**.

Army recruitment ad

leg was discovered. Now she had the pictures to go along with the pain.

But our Army-related medical problems began long before the war in Iraq. My daughter contracted Lyme disease while on one of her two-weeks-a-summer National Guard stints. The Army doctor caught it right away, but it proved intractable. Her bones were weakened by the disease, which made them brittle and easily broken. By the time she went to Iraq, she had been trying to get the Army to pay for the treatment for almost two years, since she had contracted the disease on active duty. Records were mysteriously "lost," and treatment was impossible to get because we don't have an Army medical base in our state. The closest one is located in Fort Lewis, Washington. Service-related injuries are supposed to be treated at Army bases; and the Army normally does not provide funds for any treatment by private doctors.

In the past, National Guard and reserve members were not eligible for the same medical care on bases or the same insurance for off-base treatment that regular Army soldiers are. Only conditions that

occur on active duty, such as during the one-weekend-a-month service or the two-weeks-a-year service, could be treated. Once citizen soldiers began to return from Iraq with wounds and illness, they had to remain on active duty upon their return to gain treatment at Army bases.

After my daughter was medically evacuated from Iraq, the military's push to get rid of her began. It was obvious she could not return to active duty and be redeployed to Iraq. They realized she was now just an expense, not an asset. First, the military told her she couldn't go home unless she signed a waiver releasing the Army from medical liability after ninety days.

This put her in an unusual bind. Her civilian job as a mechanic in an Army shop was dual status, which means that it was dependent on her military service. She went to war and was injured, but then, if declared disabled, upon her return she would also be fired from her civilian job because she would not be able to go back to war or perform her civilian duties any more. This was double jeopardy of the worst sort and a sorry thank-you for her military service. In addition, she would lose her

medical insurance, leaving her disabled without a safety net.

She refused to sign the papers and requested medical care on base as an injured active-duty soldier. She fought six months just to get her orders extended and to receive psychological counseling for the nightmares, anger, and anxiety.

Because many states don't have active-duty military bases, citizen soldiers are sent far away from home to receive treatment. My daughter was placed at a military base in Colorado, almost a thousand miles away from our home in Oregon. I flew to visit her as often as possible. My sister and my best friend rotated visits with me so that my daughter wouldn't be alone. Friends and relatives sent money to keep me afloat.

I wasn't the only one struggling financially.

While my daughter was on the base in Colorado, she still had to pay rent on her home in Oregon because she had a house full of goods and three dogs who needed a home. There was no housing on the medical base for her so she had to pay rent on an apartment in Colorado too. The months passed and the expenses rose for both of us.

My daughter and I became depressed by the long separation. For almost a year while she was in Iraq, the prospect of seeing and holding each other again was the one thought that kept us going. Yet here she was in the United States and we were still apart.

Finally, I saw my U.S. congressman, Peter DeFazio, on the Oregon State University campus, and I homed in on him like a heat-seeking missile. He promised to help us and he was good to his word. He immediately sent my daughter a handwritten letter, and put us in contact with his veteran's representative. DeFazio, who deserves a medal himself for what he has done for our soldiers, asked me to write a letter he could take to Congress, to seek help for my daughter.

I called the GI Rights Hotline, a privately funded organization dedicated to informing soldiers about their rights, and asked what our rights were and what we could expect from the military. Then I wrote those expectations in our letter. I wrote what it was like to be a mother, separated from my daughter in terrible times. I wrote about the pain of incessant worrying that the next phone call would be a bad one, of the terror I felt every time the doorbell rang.

I guess the letter worked. Maybe all those speeches and newspaper interviews I gave over the course of two years did too.

The secretary of the Army (probably the secretary's secretary, actually) wrote a letter to the administrators in charge of my daughter's medical care. Right before Christmas 2004, she was sent home. It was the first time she had been home since February 14, 2003. She was reassigned to a medical holdover unit in California, and allowed to stay home on extended leave.

Her active-duty status was extended so that she would be medically treated as a full-time soldier would. Because there is no base in Oregon, she was allowed to see civilian doctors and psychiatrists so that she would not have to travel to another state to be treated. After almost two entire years, she finally underwent surgery and has regular physical therapy and counseling. She is treated like any soldier who sacrificed so much to fulfill her commitment to our country ought to be.

Now the rest of the battle begins. The eight weeks after her leg was broken with no treatment rendered it irreparable, we learned after the surgery.

She will never be able to do the job she once did. My formerly athletic daughter will never be able to run, ride a bike, or hike again. Even walking is incredibly painful for her.

The Army is taking good care of her right now, but it will take months or years to gain disabled status. Once she is declared disabled, the future will remain murky. If her disability rating is low, she will not receive enough payment to support her.

My daughter and I are far from alone in our fight to get care. Many of us struggle to make ends meet while our loved ones are far from home, held up by a system that has no plan in place for them.

Most citizen soldiers get discouraged by the long wait for treatment and medical status. They sign away their right to medical care just to get home. They give up and try to deal with their disability through civilian channels, leaving the military off the hook.

If you belong to the National Guard or reserves, there is no plan in place if you become injured, maimed, or mentally wounded and disabled. Soldiers in the regular Army have a hospital on a base where they receive treatment and are housed and fed. Their big problem then is keeping doctors (under pressure from officers) from decreeing that they are well and can be sent back to combat. One friend's son, who is in the regular Army, was returned to Iraq as a gunner with a cast on his leg.

It's not much easier for those who aren't returned to combat. An October 2005 article in the *Washington Post* reported that the military has taken money from soldiers' wages to repay their combat-related debts. The military harassed one soldier, who lost his arm in combat, to repay $2,200 for travel expenses related to care, $2,400 in combat pay he was not supposed to have received, and hundreds of dollars for equipment that was missing since his injury. Once that debt was forgiven, the military began hassling him for $646 he owed for housing.

"They call and they call and they call," the soldier told the *Post*. "They're nasty to me. I don't know how much [they] want from me. I already gave [them] one arm and a part of a leg."[1]

---

1. St. George, Donna. "For Injured U.S. Troops, 'Financial Friendly Fire.'" *Washington Post,* October 14, 2005.

Recruiters make many promises to young people. What they don't tell them is that they are disposable equipment that can be discarded when its usefulness is over. They don't tell them that if they are injured they will have to fight every inch to make sure they get what they are entitled to.

Information is power. People who are about to enlist in the armed forces need fair, honest information regarding the consequences they may incur during their time in service and the hidden costs of that service. The people of America need honest information about the treatment of their heroes. For every soldier missing a leg who has a hero's welcome, there are dozens more fighting just to get fair treatment and struggling to survive without a livelihood.

I got killed in Vietnam, I just didn't know it at the time.

—Paul Reutershan, Vietnam veteran who blamed his fatal stomach cancer on Agent Orange

5

You may suffer long-term health problems

Tod Ensign

Tod Ensign, an attorney, is director of Citizen Soldier, a nonprofit GI and veterans rights advocacy organization founded during the Vietnam War. His most recent book is America's Military Today *(The New Press). He has written two other books and numerous magazine and newspaper articles discussing various problems faced by active duty GIs and military veterans.*

Airman Ed Robins's experience with the nuclear testing program was typical. A nineteen-year-old enlisted man in 1953, he knew nothing about it when his unit was sent to Nevada. Arriving at the rustic desert camp, Ed and the others were given no film badges to measure radiation exposure.

They were told that there was no danger from the nuclear bomb and that they must never tell anyone about the bomb test they witnessed.

At dawn, the men descended into shallow trenches just a few miles from "ground zero." Then the bomb, which was similar in size to that dropped on Japan, was detonated. Although Ed remained in the military until retirement, no one ever contacted him or conducted any follow-up about his post-test health history, even though radiation exposure is now known to have potentially lethal effects.[1]

During the Vietnam War, the United States used chemical weapons on a massive scale for the first time in a guerilla war. Because there were no fixed battle lines or secure territory, the military sprayed thirteen million gallons of Agent Orange herbicide over southern Vietnam. Its purpose was to kill foliage to deny cover to the insurgents and to destroy crops they could use. One of the chemicals in Agent Orange contained trace amounts of TCDD dioxin—the most toxic chemical known to science.

---

1. Author's interview with Robins's widow.

Army recruitment ad

It has been shown to cause birth defects and cancers in lab animals when administered in parts per billion![2]

After a bitter fifteen-year political battle, Congress finally ordered the VA to provide automatic disability assistance to Vietnam vets who suffered from any one of thirteen illnesses that can be caused by Agent Orange, including soft tissue cancer, non-Hodgkin's lymphoma, and multiple myeloma. Unfortunately, during the years it took to win these benefits many veterans died, and their children are still denied compensation for all but one birth defect.

Soldiers on today's battlefields still risk long-term health effects from a broad range of dangers, from bombs and bullets to chemical, biological, and nuclear weapons. And as we shall see, more psychological casualties may be produced by America's current war in Iraq than in any of its previous wars.

---

2. Uhl, Michael, and Tod Ensign. *GI Guinea Pigs*. New York: Playboy Press, 1980.

The First Gulf War:
The Toll Mounts

The first Gulf War, which took place in the Persian Gulf a decade and a half ago, gives us a sense of what to expect from the current Iraq war. Nearly 700,000 American troops were sent to the region in 1991 to oust Iraq from its occupation of Kuwait. Many of them were exposed to a variety of environmental hazards in addition to the normal dangers of war. Two-thirds of these veterans have since sought VA health care and nearly 200,000 of them receive VA disability—twice the rate for vets from World War II, Korea, or Vietnam.[3]

One of the biggest debacles of this short war was the American command's decision to blow up tons of captured Iraqi chemical weapons at Khamisiyah, Iraq. Oblivious to the hazard, these detonations rained down fallout from sarin and cyclosarin—both deadly chemical agents—on 100,000 U.S. troops.[4]

---

3. Author's interview with government source who requested anonymity (October 2005). The source risks dismissal if identified.
4. Funk, Deborah. "Gulf War's Poison Puzzle." *Army Times,* March 11, 2002.

"They took what I considered a perfectly healthy all-American boy and turned him into a crippled old man. I have illnesses that old people have," Desert Storm vet Brian Martin of Niles, Michigan, told PBS *Frontline* in October 1997. When he got home, he suffered from excruciating headaches, constant diarrhea and vomiting, poor vision, swollen limbs, and other assorted ailments.

When Martin was first examined at a VA hospital, he noticed that someone had written "exposed to chemicals" on his records. After a long struggle, Martin was finally awarded 100 percent VA disability. The media has dubbed him the "Khamisiyah kid" because of his tireless efforts as a whistleblower on this issue.

As veterans filed disability claims based on these exposures over the next several years, both the Pentagon and the CIA tried to conceal their criminal stupidity by concocting flawed fallout data. After several congressional investigations, these agencies were eventually forced to admit that many of these veterans had been recklessly exposed to toxic fallout.

Two VA-funded health studies have confirmed

that compared with non-Gulf vets, veterans of the first Gulf War suffer from a doubled rate of deadly ALS (Lou Gehrig's disease)[5] as well as twice the death rate from brain cancer.[6] Some scientists suspect that exposure to chemical weapons has contributed to these elevated rates. It's noteworthy that fifteen years later, over half of all Khamisiyah veterans have filed disability claims with the VA.[7]

Depleted Uranium: Wonder Weapon or Toxic Hazard?

The first Gulf War also marked the first time the U.S. military used tank shells and A-10 jet shells tipped with depleted uranium (DU). DU is a waste product generated by nuclear weapons and power facilities. The extreme density of this metal and its susceptibility to spontaneous burning enables it to punch and burn through conventional

---

5. Gardner, Amanda. "Gulf War Link to Lou Gehrig's Disease Bolstered." Health On the Net Foundation, September 22, 2003.

6. Funk, Deborah. "Study Links Cancer, Weapons Detonation." *Army Times,* September 12, 2005.

7. Confidential government source who would risk dismissal if identified.

armor plating. The Pentagon loves this weapon because it can penetrate almost any barrier. DU shells cut through steel or concrete as if they're butter.

But there is a downside: up to 70 percent of the DU vaporizes into fine dust upon impact, spewing clouds of microscopic particles into the air. If inhaled, these can lodge in the lungs or other organs, irradiating tissue. DU is also a highly toxic "heavy metal." Although there is some debate about its radioactivity, no one questions its chemical toxicity. According to Thomas Fasey, a pathologist who has tested some Gulf vets exposed to DU, it can bond with the body's DNA, with trace amounts causing cancers and fetal abnormalities in veterans' children.[8] Some New York National Guard members returned from Iraq with a host of new health problems: chronic fatigue, severe headaches, numbness, and joint pain. One member of the unit, Sergeant Hector Vega of the Bronx, now suffers

8. Lindorff, David. "Radioactive Wounds of War." *In These Times*, August 25, 2005.

from chest pain, heart palpitations, urinary problems, body tremors, and breathlessness.

"There were burnt-out Iraqi tanks on flatbed trucks 100 yards from where we slept," Sergeant Vega told a *Vanity Fair* reporter. "It looked like our barracks had also been hit, with black soot on the walls. It was open to the elements, and dust was coming in all the time. When the wind blew, we were eating it, breathing it."[9]

Before heading to Iraq he worked with an NYPD street narcotics team, said Sergeant Raymond Ramos of Queens, New York, another unit member. "The shape I came back in, I cannot perform at that level. I've lost forty pounds. I'm frail."[10]

During the first Gulf war, the United States released an estimated 300 tons of DU in Iraq and Kuwait. The current wars in Iraq and Afghanistan have seen a dramatic increase in the use of DU shells, with roughly 3,000 tons already expended

---

9. Rose, David. "Weapons of Self-Destruction." *Vanity Fair,* December 2004.
10. Ibid.

in the Gulf and another 1,000 tons in Afghanistan. The military has also developed a new "bunker busting" bomb that releases a thousand pounds of DU with each explosion.[11]

So far, there's been almost no research into the health risks from DU exposure. Yet again, the military is carelessly requiring soldiers to use weapons that could potentially result in lifelong medical problems.

In These Times journalist David Lindorff wrote, "The Pentagon continues to insist, on the basis of no field evidence, that DU is safe. To date, only some 270 returned troops have been tested for DU contamination by the military or the VA. But even these tests, mostly urine sampling, are useless 30 days after exposure, because by that time most of the DU will have left the body or migrated to the bones and organs."[12]

---

11. Lindorff, David. "Radioactive Wounds of War." *In These Times,* August 25, 2005.
12. Ibid.

Is the Cure Worse than the Disease?

During the first Gulf War, the Pentagon ordered tens of thousands of GIs to take two experimental drugs: anthrax vaccine and pyridostigmine bromide (PB). More than 150,000 soldiers received injections of anthrax vaccine in the hope that they would be protected if the enemy used anthrax weapons. It was thought that the PB pills would protect GIs if soman, a deadly chemical, were released on the battlefield. Almost 300,000 soldiers took this untested antidote.

After the war ended, studies revealed that neither would have provided GIs any protection. The anthrax vaccine had been designed to protect farm workers from anthrax spores found in animal skins. But typically, anthrax weapons spread their poison through aerosols that are inhaled, not by skin contact. A subsequent VA study found that PB pills actually increased soldiers' risk because when PB interacts with other chemicals its toxic effects may register at far lower doses than they would otherwise.[13]

Soldiers on active duty today must give their consent before they can be given anthrax vaccine shots. This is because a federal judge upheld a GI's claim that the vaccine is "experimental" and potentially harmful. Nonetheless, because of pressure from their commanders, about half of GIs today accept the vaccine.

Invisible Injuries: War Trauma

Thousands of Iraq and Afghanistan vets are returning home badly wounded by psychological trauma as well. Military officials estimate that up to 30 percent of all soldiers who serve in Iraq will suffer some level of mental trauma.[14]

In July 2004, the *New England Journal of Medicine* reported that 17 percent of the Iraq war vets

---

13. Golomb, Dr. Beatrice A. "A Review of Scientific Literature as It Pertains to Gulf War Illness; Vol. 2, Pyridostigmine Bromide." RAND, National Research Defense Institute (1999), p. 267.
14. Guthrie, Julian. "Iraq War Vets Fight an Enemy at Home." *San Francisco Chronicle*, January 17, 2005.

interviewed showed signs of post-traumatic stress disorder (PTSD). This finding probably understates the problem, because the researchers interviewed vets from the early stages of the occupation when fighting was less intense. They also weren't permitted to interview any hospitalized vets or any whose military tours had been involuntarily extended by Bush's "stop-loss" orders. (Read more about the stop-loss policy in chapter 9.) As of July 2005, 16,000 Iraq and Afghanistan war vets are receiving PTSD disability.[15]

Flashbacks and intense nightmares are common symptoms of PTSD. Sufferers often resort to alcohol or drug abuse in an effort to get some relief. PTSD can also trigger uncontrollable rage coupled with depression, which sufferers follow by acts of violence against others or themselves.

Just nine days after returning from Iraq in 2005, Private First Class Stephen Sherwood of Fort Collins, Colorado, killed his wife and then himself,

15. Analysis of VA Healthcare Among SE Asian War Vets, VHA office of Public Health and Environmental Hazards, Washington, DC.

orphaning their fifteen-month-old daughter.[16] Days earlier, another Iraq vet, Matthew Sepi, fired on two strangers in Las Vegas, killing one of them. Sepi told police that his Iraq experiences influenced his response to what he thought was an ambush.

Sepi's family said that he seemed different after Iraq. He would talk about the "weird noises" children make when they're dying. His request for psychiatric help from the VA had not yet been granted at the time of the shooting.[17]

American political leaders continue to send off our soldiers to fight foreign wars with brass bands and patriotic speeches that warn about "terrorism." However, when they return home with undiagnosed illnesses and chronic health problems, they receive much less attention or political support.

As we have seen, America has a history of squandering billions on these wars only to close

---

16. Gutierrez, Hector. "Soldier Found Return 'Hard.'" *Rocky Mountain News,* August 5, 2005.

17. Curreri, Frank, and Keith Rogers. "Iraq Veteran Arrested in Killing." *Las Vegas Review-Journal,* August 2, 2005.

its purse when the bill for our veterans' medical treatment is presented.

In 1950, the U.S. Supreme Court ruled in the *Feres* case that the military can never be held liable for injuries suffered while on active duty, no matter how negligent its conduct. For more than a half-century, both Congress and the high court have refused to budge from this policy. This leaves the injured veteran with only one remedy: the VA system.

One might think that the Pentagon would worry that neglecting veterans' needs would undermine its recruiting efforts, but this doesn't appear to be the case. Most soldiers still enlist primarily because they need the pay, bonuses, and college aid—deficient health care seems to be too abstract a concern.

Clearly, providing for the health needs of returning veterans ranks low on our government's list of priorities. America's vets are treated like so many soda cans; once the contents are consumed, they're tossed on to the scrap heap.

You're at war right here at home. You can get shot anywhere.

—A National Guard recruiter talking to high school students in Georgia (*Atlanta Journal-Constitution*, October 4, 2005)

If the purpose of the GI Bill is to get veterans into school, it is not accomplishing the task.

—Congressional Commission on Service-members and Veterans' Transition Assistance, 1999

In war, truth is the first casualty.

—Aeschylus

6

You may be lied to
Elizabeth Weill-Greenberg

Elizabeth Weill-Greenberg is a journalist based in Washington, D.C. She has written for the Washington Blade, In These Times, Common Dreams, *and* The Brooklyn Rail. *Elizabeth has worked as a community organizer on many criminal justice issues, like the death penalty, the prison industrial complex, and the case of political prisoner Mumia Abu-Jamal.*

"It's either jail or the military," said Jeannel Bishop, a senior at Brooklyn's South Shore High School and counter-recruitment activist. Many students at her school think enlisting is their best option.

When Navy recruiters visited South Shore,

students were allowed to leave class to meet with them. Jeannel brought pamphlets and confronted the recruiters about their assurances of tuition and training. She pointed out to them and other students nearby that getting college money was a much more complicated and uncertain process.

"I was taking over their whole show," Jeannel said. "[The recruiters] were amazed."

Three students who had been "pumped up about the military" had second thoughts after Jeannel spoke. It took just a little information for them to have doubts, she said.

After speaking with several students like Jeannel and American soldiers, I decided to see recruiters' tactics firsthand. When I posed as a potential recruit, I stayed as close to the truth as possible.

I told them I was temping as a secretary in a doctor's office for $8.00 an hour. I had no health insurance, and I was about $60,000 in debt from student loans. All of this was true. Some small lies were necessary, though. I said I was twenty-one (I was twenty-five at the time) and had completed three years of college (I have a master's degree). Most

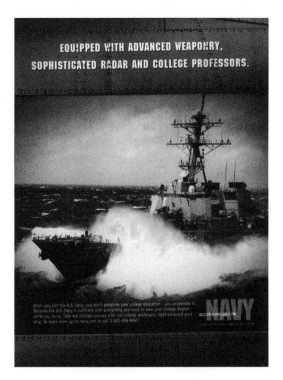

Navy recruitment ad

importantly, the recruiters knew that I, like so many of their young targets, had financial troubles.

When I met with the recruiters in their downtown Manhattan office, they kept holding out their golden ring: money.

Sergeant Preto sat to my right, Sergeant Mack to my left.[1] Preto barraged me with promises that the Army would make me financially secure. It would cancel my debt. If I went back to school, the Army would pay 100 percent of my tuition. I would work until 4:30 and go to school at night. Full medical and dental . . . Thirty days paid vacation . . . Unlimited sick days . . . Live rent free.

He pulled out a chart divided into a hundred little boxes. He pointed to the numbers in the boxes and showed how my pay would go up and up and up. I'd earn about $1,400 a month, with all living expenses covered. His friend was earning $60,000–$70,000 after he left the Army. He said soldiers had received a 20 percent raise since Bush was in office.

"What other job would promise you'd be debt

---

1. Names of recruiters have been changed.

free, fully insured, and making $1,400 a month?" he asked.

But when I hesitated, he asked why.

"I'm just really concerned about going into combat."

"So you're scared?" he teased. "That's the first thing you mentioned—'I don't want to go to combat.'"

He pointed to Sergeant Mack: "He went for five months." And then he pointed to a recruiter across the room: "He went for a year. They went. They're OK."

The mocking continued. He asked if I had an 8:00 curfew in high school. He said I was probably the sort of kid who was locked in my house on a Friday night.

They asked me a few other questions about my limited athletic abilities and drug history. If asked if I had ever smoked pot, lie and say no, they instructed.

As I sat in the office, several teenagers who looked about eighteen or nineteen walked through. All were either black or Latino. Each was greeted warmly and with affection.

Finally, it was time to meet Sergeant Suarez—the "closer." He was a smiling, flamboyant, well-groomed man with carefully gelled hair and a weak handshake. He told me he grew up in Puerto Rico in a blue-collar household. He now had a college degree, he said, pulling out a white binder and flipping to a plastic-covered diploma. He had two houses. He had traveled all over the world.

At one point Suarez asked me, in classic car salesman mode, "What can I do to get your name on this [agreement]?" Like all salespeople, recruiters are under intense pressure to meet their quotas. The 2006 Defense Authorization bill proposes a $1,000 finder's fee for soldiers who successfully refer new recruits to military recruiters.

He told me I could choose any job I wanted, provided their test qualified me. If I didn't get the job I picked, he would get on the phone and make sure I did. I could travel to Germany, Hawaii, Alaska.

Wait. Stop right there. Would recruiters really need to lie, harass, and push their way into public schools if they just gave out all-expense paid trips to Hawaii and gobs of college money?

The truth is that most people who sign up for the military aren't going to Germany, Hawaii, or Alaska. They're going to Iraq. The *Los Angeles Times* reported that half the recruits going through Fort Benning in Georgia will be deployed to Iraq or Afghanistan thirty days after finishing basic training. The rest will likely go during their first enlistment.[2]

I told Suarez that my mom was worried about my going into combat.

"You could get shot—God forbid—in front of your apartment. More people were killed in New York last week than Iraq," he said repeating one of the recruiters' favorite mantras.

Recruiters will do or say just about anything to convince young people that the Army is not about war. No, the military isn't all guns and tears and pain. It's hip, cool, rebellious even. (My recruiter told me to "cut the umbilical cord" when I said I didn't think my mom would approve.)

Recruiters will prey on any opening they have to

2. Fiore, Faye. "Every Enlistee First a Warrior." *Los Angeles Times*, November 29, 2004.

young people—including military-sponsored video games and rock concerts, soliciting outside malls, accessing private information through testing, offering free iTunes, as well as by exploiting kids' boredom and frustrations.

But no place is quite as fertile for recruiters as public schools. Under No Child Left Behind, public schools have to turn over their students' private information or they risk losing federal funds. Students can "opt-out," but most schools don't publicize this option and recruiters find other ways of getting in.

The 2004 guidebook for high school recruiters offers detailed instructions on how to gain the trust of students and teachers:

- Know your student influencers. Students such as class officers, newspaper and yearbook editors, and athletes can help build interest in the Army among the student body.

- Attend athletic events at the HS. Make sure you wear your uniform.

- Deliver donuts and coffee for the faculty once a month.

- Coordinate with the homecoming committee to get involved with the parade.

- Get involved with local Boy Scout troops. . . . Many scouts are HS students and potential enlistees or student influencers.

- Offer to be a timekeeper at football games.

- Contact the HS athletic director and arrange for an exhibition basketball game between the faculty and Army recruiters.[3]

Recruiters don't put that time and energy into every school. They go to schools with students from poor and working-class backgrounds, where young people want a way out but don't see any.

The National Priorities Project found that in 2004 almost two-thirds of recruits were from counties with median household incomes below the U.S. median. Seventy-five percent of the top twenty counties with the highest number of

_____

3. School Recruiting Program Handbook. USAREC Pamphlet 350–13, http://rncwatch.typepad.com/counterrecruiter/ SchoolRecruitingProgramHandbook.pdf.

recruits had higher poverty rates than the national average.[4]

The New York Civil Liberties Union publicized training materials from the Defense Department's Joint Advertising and Marketing Research and Studies Web site, which explicitly targets black and Latino youth. One section details the obstacles of recruiting black teens, such as widespread opposition to the war in the black community and well-known hip-hop artists speaking out against the war.

The marketing report states:

- Because of this influence, the Hip-Hop community's negative views about the war in Iraq are also influencing their thinking on this subject.

- As a result, there is a need for the military to enlist other influencers and employ the best direct marketing vehicles to engage prospects and help counteract this view.[5]

---

4. Military Recruitment in FY 2004 Overview. The National Priorities Project, November 1, 2005.

5. "Marketing to Hispanics" and "Marketing to African Americans." Joint Advertising and Marketing Research and Studies Web site, www.jamrs.org.

There may be no better example of recruiters' exploitation of hopelessness than Hurricane Katrina. In the aftermath, the *Wall Street Journal* reported, military recruiters were in the Astrodome, urging folks who had lost everything to sign up.[6]

These recruiters offer what society doesn't—money for college, a promising future, and a fulfilling career. Why is it that lower income people have to risk their lives for these opportunities?

And once you sign up, recruiters' seductive promises often evaporate.

The DOD Enlistment/Reenlistment contract says: "Laws and regulations that govern military personnel may change without notice to me. Such changes may affect my status, pay, allowances, benefits and responsibilities."

Kim's son didn't expect to see combat when he signed up. The recruiter told him he could pick a job in accounting, but once he was in, the only jobs open to him were in infantry. He was sent to Iraq.

"My son, Josh, was lied to by the recruiters—by

6. Harwood, John. "Louisiana Lawmakers Aim to Cope with Political Fallout." *Washington Wire,* September 9, 2005.

the government—from beginning to end," Kim told me at an antiwar protest in Harlem. "My son doesn't understand why we're there. He tells me, 'I'm only nineteen. I haven't lived yet and I'm already facing the possibility I might not come home.'"

Countless recruits who were told they would never see combat are shipped to Iraq. This includes people who signed up for the National Guard—so-called weekend warriors who are supposed to work at home, helping with disaster relief.

As of October 2005, about one-quarter of American soldiers' deaths in Iraq have been National Guard and reservists. The Guard and Reserves have not been so widely used in combat since World War II.[7]

And what about those promises of college tuition and job training?

Well, as Vice President Dick Cheney reportedly said, "The reason to have a military is to be

---

7. Wagner, Daniel. "The Fallen 2,000; Portraits of the Casualties of War; The Death Rolls Show Military Much Changed since Vietnam—Troops Are Older, More Likely to Have Spouses, Kids." *Newsday,* October 26, 2005.

prepared to fight and win wars. . . . It's not a jobs program."[8]

Just to qualify for the Montgomery GI Bill soldiers have to pay $100 a month for a year—and that is still no guarantee they'll have their college tuition covered. If a soldier serves at least three years and is honorably discharged, then he or she is eligible to receive up to $985 a month for thirty-six months—a total of $32,000.[9] As of 2005, four years for an in-state student at Rutgers University costs $72,540. For an in-state student at Indiana University, four years costs $50,912–57,104.

According to Tod Ensign's book, *America's Military Today,* 15 percent of those who use the GI Bill earn four-year college degrees. To qualify for that $50,000 splattered on the Army ads, recruits have to sign up for infantry, armor, or artillery—which greatly diminishes their chances of making it to college in one piece, or at all.[10]

---

8. Central Committee for Conscientious Objectors, http://www.objector.org.

9. Ensign, Tod. *America's Military Today*. New York: The New Press, 2004.

10. Ibid.

And the recruiters mocked me for being scared of going to Iraq?

As of this writing, more than 2,000 American soldiers have been killed in Iraq and more than 30,000 have been injured.[11]

The *New England Journal of Medicine* reported that about one in six soldiers returning from Iraq experience mental health problems.[12] Military families are often abandoned by the Army and forced to fight for proper medical care, as well as deal with the financial pressures of deployment, extended tours, and illness. And don't look to the Bush administration for help. They've tried to cut funding to VA hospitals and soldiers' combat pay.

But in the recruiter's shiny office there was no mention of death or injury or killing. Instead,

---

11. *60 Minutes*, "Iraq: The Uncounted." November 21, 2004 Department of Defense, http://www.defenselink.mil.news/casualty.pdf.

12. Hoge, Charles W. et al. "Combat Duty in Iraq and Afghanistan, Mental Health Problems, and Barriers to Care." *New England Journal of Medicine*, July 1, 2004.

they offered me a way out of a dead-end job and overpriced New York rents. For every problem I had, they had a solution.

Needless to say, the truth is not an effective recruiting tool.

Whenever I meet any young man, whether he be black, white, Hispanic, whatever I let him know that he does have options 'cause I didn't have anyone telling me that, so I let him know how to join the Army.

—Sgt. Bryan Randall in an Army recruitment ad that refers to him as "The Hip Hop Soldier"

7

You may face discrimination
Aimee Allison

Aimee Allison served as a medic in the Army Reserves and received an honorable discharge as a conscientious objector during the Persian Gulf War. A community activist and organizational consultant, she counsels military people seeking CO discharges and is a leader in the counter-recruitment movement.

I desperately wanted out of my small-minded hometown of Antioch, California, and the military recruiter on my high school campus promised me an escape hatch. The family that my white mother and African American father created was based on the belief that the hard work and democratic values of 1960s activists made equality my birthright. But my day-to-day experience was full of evidence that racism was alive and well. High school classmates would chant the n-word when our team played its biggest rival the next town over. Slurs against gay people were so accepted that teachers used them without thought. And after winning a local Junior Miss competition, a first for a black contestant, I was excluded from the local news and town parade. When I brought my Ivy League college acceptance letter into the career center, a counselor suggested that I got in because of my race.

So I rushed to sign up for the Army Reserves, in part because it was the only place I knew of that promised I wouldn't be judged or limited by my race or gender. We women, people of color, and immigrants are especially attracted by the idea that we could live our lives on equal footing with other Americans. But the military isn't the egalitarian nirvana that its multi-billion dollar advertising blitz—with a budget of almost $4 billion in 2003—claims.[1]

---

1. Merrow, John. "High School Recruiting." *Online News Hour*, December 13, 2004.

Army recruitment ad

Like most female soldiers, I learned the hard way that men dominate military culture. We are stuck in a system that makes it difficult to report abuse because of fear of reprisal. Even the military itself admitted in a June 2005 report by the Defense Task Force on Sexual Harassment and Violence at the Military Service Academies, "harassment is the more prevalent and corrosive problem, creating an environment in which sexual assault is more likely to occur."[2]

Just ask any woman in uniform—sexual harassment is a common experience on base. I remember on the day of boot camp graduation, the same drill sergeant who had threatened to "rip off my head and shit in my neck" for a minor infraction during training grabbed my arm in the on-base store and pressured me for a date. This was a man that had exercised incredible power over me and my unit for twelve weeks, and through my fear I mumbled, "Drill sergeant, no" three times before

---

2. Report of the Defense Task Force on Sexual Harassment and Violence at the Military Service Academies. http://www.dtic.mil/dtfs, June 2005.

he let me go. I didn't know at the time that about 60 percent of women who have served in the National Guard and reserves said they were sexually harassed or assaulted, but less than one-quarter reported it. Many who did complain were encouraged to drop their complaints.[3]

When I first joined the military at age seventeen, a military doctor administered a demeaning and uncomfortable pelvic exam during my induction physical. He didn't wear gloves. It turns out that my experience wasn't unusual.

At last year's National Summit of Women Veterans Issues in Washington, D.C., former Air Force officer Dorothy Mackey told of several instances of abuse during OB-GYN exams. "He sodomized me," she said. "I started looking into what happens in a normal OB-GYN examination, and that is definitely not supposed to be part of it."[4]

Nine out of ten women under fifty who had

---

3. Baldor, Lolita. "Reservists Allege Sex Harassment." Associated Press, September 29, 2005.

4. Lydersen, Kari. "Rape Nation." AlterNet, http://www.alternet.org/rights/19134, July 2, 2004.

served in the U.S. military and had responded to a survey reported being sexually harassed while in the service.[5] In an episode of *60 Minutes,*[6] New Jersey National Guard Lieutenant Jennifer Dyer revealed that she was treated like a criminal after accusing a fellow officer of rape in early 2004. She reported the rape immediately to the military criminal investigation division (CID), who took her to a civilian hospital for a rape kit—then held her in seclusion for the next three days with no counseling and no medical treatment. The CID agent advised her of her Miranda rights and threatened to prosecute her for filing a false report. Her command announced her rape and accusation to the entire unit. By the time she returned to her unit after a two-week leave, she was "fearful for [her]

5. Murdoch, Maureen, and Kristin Nicole. "Women Veterans' Experience with Domestic Violence and with Sexual Harassment while in the Military." *Archives of Family Medicine,* May 1995.

6. "Army Rape Accuser Speaks Out." http://www.cbsnews .com/stories/2005/02/17/60minutes/main674791.shtml, February 20, 2005.

health, safety, and sanity." Her assailant was roaming free on base and was later acquitted of any crime.

All the bad press about rape in the military has led to congressional demands for reform. For the eighteenth time in sixteen years, the Pentagon has studied the problem and proposed changes, including designated victim advocates in every command and a promise of confidentiality, according to *60 Minutes*.

It's too bad that fully funding this need isn't a high priority. A Department of Veterans Affairs report released in September 2005 found that the annual cost for health care, including mental health for National Guard members like Lieutenant Jennifer Dyer who experience sexual trauma, is about $20 million. Only $13 million is budgeted for the 2006 fiscal year.

Reports of sexual assaults have skyrocketed recently, especially in hostile environments like Iraq and Afghanistan. The *Washington Post* reported, "In many U.S. military camps in Iraq, for example, signs are posted in female showers and other locations requiring U.S. servicewomen to be in the company of a 'battle buddy,' especially at night, for their safety."[7]

The military has rules and structures to direct every aspect of a person's conduct. Why does abuse still occur? One answer is that a male commander most often decides when to prosecute for abuse or misconduct. In 2002, the number of female active Army officers was about 20 percent.[8] This means that the vast majority of officers in the military are men.

In addition, military training itself is responsible for further desensitizing men to sexual violence. In January 2003, the *Village Voice* reported that military training has included efforts to get young soldiers used to the sounds of women being raped so that, if captured, hearing fellow soldiers assaulted would not cause them to crack.[9]

---

7. Tyson, Ann. "Reported Cases of Sexual Assault in Military Increase." *Washington Post,* May 7, 2005.

8. "Population Representation in the Military Services." Department of Defense, 2003.

9. Baard, Erik. "The Guilt-Free Soldier." *The Village Voice,* January 2003, 22–28.

These revelations are not surprising to former Marine Corps Lance Corporal Stephen Funk. During his training in 2002, Stephen told me that his drill instructor gave a rousing speech at the end of Marine combat training: "This is the reality of war. We Marines like war. We like killing. We like raping females. This is what we do." If there was a touch of irony in his voice, it sure wasn't clear to the young, impressionable group eager to prove they were men, Stephen said.

Basic training also reinforces racism. Boot camp systematically breaks a recruit down physically and emotionally. Military discipline depends on eliminating individuality. Anything that makes you different from the "standard" (read: straight white male) makes you a target for abuse. But submissiveness and conformity are not the only goals of training. Soldiers are taught to follow orders in war without question. When the training taps into a person's own racist views, it's easier to convince them to kill people who are different.

Iraq war veteran Aidan Delgado, who served as a mechanic in the 320th Military Police Company in Abu Ghraib, described how his training led to racism against Muslims and Arabs.

" 'Hajji' is the new slur, the new ethnic slur for Arabs and Muslims. It is used extensively in the military," he told a reporter. "The Arabic word refers to one who has gone on a pilgrimage to Mecca. But it is used in the military with the same kind of connotation as 'gook,' 'Charlie,' or the n-word."[10]

Stephen, the former Marine corporal, said that his training on operating machine guns included a tip to avoid overheating the machinery: Squeeze the trigger for as long as it takes to chant, "Die, fucking raghead, die." When riling up the troops to take part in a nighttime simulation, the squad leader would yell, Stephen recalled, "Let's go burn some turbans!"

But racism in the military doesn't stop at Arabs. Basic training—a nightmare for most—is even more difficult if you happen to be a person of color

---

10. Rockwell, Paul. "Army Reservist Witnesses War Crimes: New Revelations about Racism in the Military." *In Motion Magazine*, April 2, 2005.

or gay. If you are in these groups, I don't have to tell you that many times it's seemingly small insults that create a feeling of oppression.

When I was at Army boot camp at Fort Jackson, South Carolina, standing in line for chow, I overheard the white drill sergeant tell a dark-skinned recruit with a smile, "You look like Kunta Kinte [a slave from the TV miniseries *Roots*]."

"Doesn't she? Doesn't she?" he asked everyone within earshot. She moved on silently in the wake of laughter.

It was common for my drill sergeant to ask, "Where are my Chinese at?" when assigning laundry duty. "For some reason, they do it the best," he'd say with a smirk.

I went to training with many new immigrants, since recruiters often falsely promised them citizenship. One Sudanese immigrant was the butt of many of the drill sergeant's jokes. The sergeant would hand him a dark-colored rifle and then loudly comment that they couldn't tell where the rifle ended and the hands began.

In preparation for a night-ops simulation, the drill sergeant announced that recruits were to blow a whistle if they got lost. "Except you," he said, pointing at the Sudanese recruit. "You just smile and we'll see you in the dark."

Then the drill instructor made him stand up in front of the others.

"Give me a pimp walk," the instructor ordered.

English wasn't his native language and he hadn't been in the United States long, so he didn't understand what the sergeant meant. Then the sergeant pulled up another black recruit and said, "Give me a pimp walk." The man answered that he didn't know how because he wasn't a pimp. Finally, a white recruit volunteered to show the group. Pretty soon, many others were doing the "black" pimp walk as well.

In the early morning hours during the second week of boot camp, I was forced to leave my barracks with an unfamiliar drill sergeant who decided to punish me for turning my head while standing at attention. I was afraid to go with a strange man to another part of the base, but was just as scared to refuse. He made me stand at attention and gathered his unit around to watch the show. He called me stupid, ugly, dumb.

"Where are you from, private?" he screamed. "You look like a gang member. Are you a gang member?"

I started crying—he looked at my dark skin and didn't know or care that I was an excellent student on my way to the university.

"Get down into front position!" he yelled at me in front of his own unit of women. "Get up. Get down. Get up."

The thirty minutes of humiliation seemed to last an eternity.

Although the military doesn't officially condone racism and sexism, it explicitly discriminates against gays who are open about their identity, both in legal practice and in day-to-day life. The Servicemembers Legal Defense Network, an advocacy group for gay and lesbian soldiers, claims that more than 65,000 lesbian and gay Americans are on active duty and serving in the National Guard and reserves.

Thanks to the "Don't Ask, Don't Tell" policy, put in place under the Clinton administration in 1993, as long as gay people stay deep in the closet, the military won't kick them out. In other words, "Don't

Ask, Don't Tell" actually authorizes the federal government to fire someone for being gay. According to the Servicemembers Legal Defense Network Web site (www.sldn.org), soldiers may be investigated and administratively discharged if they:

- make a statement that they are lesbian, gay, or bisexual;

- engage in physical contact with someone of the same sex for the purposes of sexual gratification; or

- marry, or attempt to marry, someone of the same sex.

Several soldiers have been discharged for posting online profiles that indicated they were gay or looking to date someone of the same gender.

The other part of the "Don't Ask, Don't Tell" policy attempts to limit harassment and the scope of investigations into a soldier's sexual orientation. Yet, as Stephen Funk's experience shows, the services continue to violate these basic rules. Stephen, a gay man, told me what it's like to live with a constant barrage of antigay slurs. No one dares speak up against it because they fear facing suspicion and investigation for being gay. Stephen's sergeant secretly investigated his homosexuality for more than a month by pulling other members of his unit into his office and grilling them about his suspicions. A soldier in his squad finally told Stephen about the interview: the sergeant had asked him, "Did you notice anything 'funny'? Did he touch you or use 'gay' words? Do you agree that his feminine gestures and soft voice make him seem like a 'fag'?"

After learning about the investigation, Stephen was forever shaken and self-conscious about his interactions with other soldiers.

The military may try to sell itself as a level playing field, but as long as abuse is tolerated and discrimination helps recruits pull the trigger, they will always be part of the soldiers' experience.

The darkest places in Hell are reserved for those who maintain their neutrality in times of moral crisis.

—Dante

8

You may be asked to do things against your beliefs
Elizabeth Weill-Greenberg

More Americans disapprove of the Iraq war than support it. Fifty-three percent of people surveyed thought the war was a mistake, according to a poll conducted in late August 2005.[1] Soldiers are confronted with the dilemma of participating in a war they disagree with or risking their careers, and possibly their freedom, by saying no.

When Pablo Paredes, then an eighteen-year-old from the South Bronx, joined the Navy, he was only concerned with survival. Little did he know that a few years later he would make national news when he refused to board a ship ferrying soldiers to fight in Iraq.

---

1. Associated Press/Ipsos, August 22–24, 2005.

"I came from that survival nature where you're more worried about putting bread on the table than you are about getting As on your tests," Pablo said in a telephone interview. "If it paid for my bills, then it was important to me at that time."

On December 6, 2004, Pablo reported to the 32nd Street Naval Station in San Diego and told reporters his decision not to board.

"Here you are carrying people to their death, and to criminal actions and to murder," Pablo said of his orders that day. "I knew I wasn't going to do it. Rather than do it in a way that compromises my integrity, I'd rather just be honest about it."

Pablo began preparing a conscientious objector (CO) application and turned himself in to Naval authorities on December 18.

Like many antiwar soldiers who have come before him, his opposition developed during his time in the military.

In 2000, Pablo was working two jobs and attending college but he still couldn't afford his tuition. He considered getting a third job but, on his military recruiters' promises of educational opportunities, he opted to join the Navy instead.

Army recruitment ad

Two years later, he went to Japan, where he met people who spoke critically about U.S. military interventions. Pablo had not given much thought to political issues before; the Navy was simply a job for him.

"It pushed me to get very educated as far as political ramifications of the military, especially as a Latino," Pablo said. "It was a birth of a different identity for me."

By the time he returned to the United States in 2004, Pablo was wrestling with his participation in the military and his moral opposition to all war. To avoid any involvement with the Iraq war, he unsuccessfully tried to switch jobs to work as a military police officer, working stateside.

Pablo's new convictions were eventually tested when he was ordered to board a ship that would bring soldiers to Iraq.

"I don't want to be a part of a ship that's taking 3,000 Marines over there, knowing 100 or more of them won't come back," he told reporters on December 6, 2004. "I can't sleep at night knowing that's what I do for a living."

Pablo is joining a growing number of soldiers

who are protesting the Iraq war by refusing orders, going AWOL, fleeing to Canada, or speaking out. Unlike regular citizens, though, a soldier's protest carries risks of imprisonment.

When Camilo Mejía refused to return to Iraq and filed a CO application, he was sentenced to 1 year in a military prison; conscientious objector Kevin Benderman was sentenced to 15 months; and Pablo was sentenced to 3 months of hard labor without confinement.[2]

Despite soldiers' rising voices, many in the Defense Department dismiss the notion that there is significant resistance within the military, pointing to numbers that show desertion rates dropping from about 8,300 in 2001 to about 5,100 in 2004. But according to the Army public affairs office, CO applications have more than doubled since 2001, from twenty-three applications to sixty in 2004.

---

2. Bynum, Russ. "Objecting Soldier Gets 15 Months in Prison for Refusing Iraq Duty." Associated Press, July 29, 2005; "Staff Sergeant Camilo Mejía Castillo Is a Prisoner of Conscience." Amnesty International, June 4, 2004; www .swiftsmartveterans.com.

Military data may show desertion rates decreasing, but Steve Morse of the GI Rights Hotline says that the calls they receive illustrate a different trend—from 17,000 in 2001 to more than 32,000 in 2004. Thirty percent of their calls in 2004 were from service members who are AWOL or are thinking about deserting, he said.

Christopher Harrison, a former officer in the Army, applied to be a CO after 9/11 when he was about twenty-eight years old. He knew he had to apply to be a CO when he began having anxiety attacks before drills. In the nine years since he signed up, he became interested in trade and environmental issues, as well as an avid reader of progressive writers like Howard Zinn and Noam Chomsky. "People didn't understand why my beliefs changed," said Christopher. "I was nineteen when I signed the cadet contract. They couldn't grasp [what] happened to me."

Christopher, co-founder of a counseling network for COs called Peace-Out, warns young people who are considering a life in the military to understand the autonomy they forfeit when they enlist: "Once you sign the contract, you don't own yourself anymore."

The standard for conscientious objection is almost "unattainably high," as Christopher said, and even more difficult to get during wartime. In 2001, eighteen CO applications were approved out of twenty-three compared with thirty approved out of sixty applications in 2004, according to the Army public affairs office. To become a CO, a soldier must prove "sincerity," an intangible but essential criterion. Also, a CO has to oppose all military conflicts, not just the particular one he or she is asked to fight in. The antiwar movement has attracted many unlikely allies from across the political spectrum. But soldiers are asked to suspend thought and directly participate in a war more and more people believe is immoral and unwinnable.

The often lengthy process is just one part of the difficulty of becoming a CO. Some COs face retaliation and humiliation from fellow soldiers and officers. Chas Davis, a CO who also works with Peace-Out, said while his officers were supportive, some of his fellow soldiers and members of his own family were not.

"My aunt and uncle disowned me. They called me a coward, a quitter," he said.

Chas signed up after he dropped out of high school. "I was working freakin' dead-end, minimum-wage jobs," he said. "I had never done anything big. I was getting my life on track."

The recruiter assured him he would not get deployed and could get an education. He learned that both promises were lies. Chas was sent to a base without an educational facility and assigned to a military police unit that was one of the most often deployed.

When he joined the military, his parents, he said, "were simply proud I decided to do something with my life."

"Everybody I knew were all extremely proud of what I decided to do," he said. "The thought of letting all those people down makes your stomach sink."

Shortly after he joined, he realized the Army was not the noble profession he had imagined. He found that the military was about dehumanization of the enemy and the soldiers themselves. Chas explained that this process started in boot camp with "sick, twisted" drills, like "Sniper Wonderland:"

"See the little girl with the puppy; Lock and load a hollow pointed round. . . . Take the shot and maybe if you're lucky; You'll watch their lifeless bodies hit the ground. . . . Through the fields we'll be walkin'; 'Cross the rooftops we'll be stalkin' . . . One shot one kill from the top of the hill. . . . Walkin' in a sniper wonderland."

"You're singing these things and you know they're wrong," he said. "But if you don't say it, you'll catch so much hell. You're scared to death and you have to say it."

Following orders without question is a staple of military life. But during wartime, those orders can be unnecessarily dangerous, immoral, or illegal, as chapter 2 discusses. Soldiers in Iraq are ordered to perform missions without armored vehicles and protective gear. The situation has become so desperate that many families have been forced to buy expensive armor to send to loved ones in Iraq.

When eighteen members of a platoon refused to go on what they deemed a "suicide mission," they were arrested and the Army launched an investigation into their actions. In October 2004, the 343rd Quartermaster Company was ordered to deliver contaminated fuel to another base in Iraq. They lacked armed escorts and they'd been having trouble with their trucks, many of which were unarmored and couldn't go faster than 40 mph.[3]

"I got a call from an officer in another unit early [Thursday] morning who told me that my husband and his platoon had been arrested on a bogus charge because they refused to go on a suicide mission," said Jackie Butler of Jackson, Mississippi, Sergeant Michael Butler's wife. "When my husband refuses to follow an order, it has to be something major."[4]

One mother, Teresa Hill, also of Jackson, Mississippi, played a telephone message from her

---

3. Lumpkin, John J. "Unit Refused Iraq Mission, Military Says." Associated Press, October 18, 2004; "Soldiers Who Refused Orders Face General Discharge, Family Says." Associated Press, October 10, 2004.

4. Hudson, Jeremy. "Platoon Defies Orders in Iraq." *Mississippi Clarion-Ledger,* October 15, 2004.

twenty-one-year old daughter, one of the soldiers who refused orders: "They are holding us against our will. . . . We are now prisoners. . . . I'm not even supposed to be using the phone."[5]

Since the start of the Iraq war, I've heard about the nobility of a soldier's sacrifice—sacrificing life and limb for country. But by participating in an immoral war, by torturing and killing civilians, by putting themselves and fellow soldiers at risk because they lack proper equipment, today's soldiers are asked to sacrifice their integrity and common sense as well.

5. Katz, Celeste, and Corky Siemaszko. "Probe Iraq 'Mutiny.'" *New York Daily News,* October 16, 2004.

I am a serviceman being held against my will in Iraq, as [my tour of duty is] being extended as a part of the Army's stop-loss program.

—Matthew Banevich (letter to the editor, *Chicago Sun-Times*, June 2, 2005)

A contract is not a contract if you sign it with the military.

—Steven Goldberg, an attorney challenging the stop-loss policy (*PBS Newshour*, February 24, 2005)

9

You may find it difficult to leave the military

Louis and Marti Hiken

Louis Hiken has represented GIs in court-martials, administrative discharge hearings, and federal court proceedings for the last thirty years. He has been a member of the Steering Committee of the Military Law Task Force of the National Lawyers Guild since the 1970s. He is currently a supervising attorney with the California Appellate Project, assisting in the defense of death penalty cases pending before the California Supreme Court.

Marti Hiken, a civilian military counselor and legal worker, is currently co-chair of the Military Law Task Force. Previously, she was the associate director at the Institute for Public Accuracy. She was also the director of the NLG Prison Law Project and chaired the NLG Native American Committee in the early 1970s.

The Military Law Task Force sued the Department of Defense over its stop-loss policy, also known as the back-door draft. Stop loss, which forces soldiers to stay in the military past their enlistment date—sometimes for years—has been one of the government's ways to keep troops in Iraq.

There's an old quip that military justice is to justice as military music is to music. Here's a new one: getting out of the military is like trying to leave prison before your sentence is up.

The military does all it can to keep you in. It bends over backward, as a matter of fact. For example, the calls pour in to the Military Law Task Force (MLTF) from new enlistees who say that their recruiters told them to lie on their enlistment contracts about their mental problems, including confinements to hospitals and drugs they might be taking. Many GIs, once they decide to get out, collect medical documentation of their mental illness from civilian psychiatrists and military doctors.

Army recruitment ad

But now that they have stepped over the line into the military, the rules have changed, and it is the military that evaluates the extent and nature of their problems. Frequently, significant mental illnesses, drug addiction, and other conditions seem to disappear overnight, and the military decides that the person is not really "sick" at all.

Rumors about the possible ways to get the military to kick them out pass quickly among GIs. We have received calls from GIs who have gone so far as to shoot themselves to get discharged. In July 2005, a nineteen-year-old GI had his cousin shoot him in the leg so he wouldn't be sent back to Iraq. The military is well aware of this technique, however, and could easily charge and confine the GI for attempting to destroy military property—after all, GI stands for government issue. Not even pregnancy will guarantee a discharge, as we discovered through one expectant mother who sought help from the MLTF.

GIs are as creative and imaginative as anyone else. Some of them fake mental illness or make up excuses about sick family members or invent other fantasies. But it's very difficult for people to "hustle" their way out of the military, and unless they can document the problems they are asserting, fake excuses usually fail.

Now it's even harder to leave, since the military began its unprecedented widespread use of the stop-loss policy. Stop loss allows the military to extend a GI's discharge date indefinitely, thanks to a presidential order in 2001 asserting the existence of an "emergency" that justifies such a policy.

"John Doe" (an alias) was one of the first Iraq vets to challenge his stop-loss order in the federal district court. There are several other cases pending at various levels of the court system. There are five different claims in the stop-loss cases. One challenges the contract violation. Another challenges the right of the president to make this decision without a congressional declaration of war. A third argues that there must be a legitimate "emergency" before the president can exercise his right to invoke stop loss, or the war powers, and that Iraq is not, and never was, a legitimate threat to the United States. The other two arguments involve the legal interpretation of separation of powers and presidential authority.

John Doe was back from Iraq and ready to walk off the base with a discharge in his hand when he was stopped by a recruiter who urged him to sign up for one more year with the "Try One" program. "It'll give you the chance to try out whether you want to stay in the military. If you don't like it, well, hey man, you can still attend college while on the program, and then you can leave. You can't lose with this." So Doe signed up for one year, the Army issued a stop-loss order, and he is in for as long as the Army wants him. This also happened to Sergeant Emiliano Santiago, a plaintiff in the second stop-loss challenge. "Try One—it's only for one year," they say. Doe's and Santiago's current discharge date is 2031.

So far about 15,000 troops have had their tours extended beyond their contracts thanks to stop loss.[1] We've heard of soldiers called back to Iraq, who are now on their fourth tour of duty.

From our perspective as military counselors, it's easy to see that recruiters lie to get seventeen- or

---

1. Schmitt, Eric. "The Basics; Troops for All Wars; Appetite for Few." *New York Times*, October 23, 2005.

eighteen-year-old boys and girls to enlist. Yet people never seem to catch on. The MLTF receives a large number of calls from GIs who enlisted with the assurance that they wouldn't have to go to Iraq or Afghanistan. They didn't get the guarantee in writing, they had no witnesses to what the recruiter said, and like almost everyone else, they believed what the recruiter told them. They were pressured into signing on the dotted line with only verbal promises, and now they call and say, "What can I do? The recruiter lied to me. I want out."

One GI called to say that he was fifty-nine years old and had just received notice that he was being called up. "I really wouldn't mind being in the military again," he said. "You know, I already served years ago, got my benefits, everything. I've been out for thirty-plus years, and I'm really surprised they want me."

"Why?" we asked.

"Because I lost my leg a couple of decades ago, and you know, they say I have to show up anyway. I can't figure it."

We've got to hand it to the parents this time around with the Iraq war. The recruiters want to run out the back door when parents show up with their sons and daughters. Parents ask the difficult and embarrassing questions and don't let things slide as readily as their nineteen-year-olds would. But there's only so much they can do to protect their kids.

An immigrant mother called us at one point about her son, who was in the Marines. She wanted him out and at home to help her take care of his father. She had made multiple telephone calls to her son's commanding officer, demanding that he be released, but the military was not complying with her wishes. When we questioned her further, she admitted that her son had never told her he wanted to leave the Marines. She had presumed that in this country, if she wanted him released, the military was required to let him out immediately. "I have rights, too," she said. We were sorry to inform her that her rights as a mother did not extend to obtaining the discharge for her son.

The Louisiana National Guard returned safely from combat in Iraq just after most of their families had lost everything to Hurricane Katrina. As the GIs got off the plane, standing right there were the recruiters, saying that they all should re-up. This way they would have a livelihood. After all, they needed to support their families. But the military didn't offer them homes or money to rebuild their lives. The recruiters weren't there to help the GIs. They were there for the U.S. military—to get these combat-weary soldiers back into a war zone.

Your buddies, they need you. Your country needs you. Your family needs the income. And, as the recruiter told you, you can have any specialty you choose and you don't have to go anywhere you don't want to.

In the 1960s, GIs signed up for the same reasons—false ones, but the same ones. It took ten years before the GI resistance to the Vietnam War had progressed to the point where they started turning the guns around and "fragging" their commanding officers. (We do not advocate such extreme measures.) The military is having a tough time meeting its recruitment goals. There are not enough troops available to send to Iraq. So you can bet they aren't going to make it easy for you to get out. The best advice we can give is not to join in the first place.

The pioneers of a warless world are the youth that refuse military service.

—Albert Einstein

10

You have other choices
Rae Abileah,
with research assistance
from Jen Low

Rae Abileah is an activist, writer, and artist who considered joining the military after high school to secure much-needed funds for a college education. Rae has been active in the movement to counter military recruiters on college and high school campuses and to foster a stronger youth antiwar movement. She currently works for Code Pink: Women for Peace as the national local groups coordinator, helping to strengthen the grassroots peace movement in the United States and abroad.

When I was five years old, I made up my mind to become an astronaut. At eight, the dream had shifted to architecture. By the time I reached thirteen, my latest plan for success involved medical school—a chance to heal the sick. These aspirations came to a halt when my mother's bruised and battered relationship with my alcoholic father finally erupted, after years of her trying to hold it together. My parents' divorce ravaged not only our emotional reserves, but left all our bank accounts empty in its wake. Money that had been destined for my college tuition went into paying astronomical legal fees, and college no longer seemed like a realistic option for me. The only way to a college degree appeared to be through the military, which advertised tens of thousands of dollars for school.

The ad that tempted me to join depicted a large ship and a strong, muscular man standing next to a petite woman. The caption read something like, "This Coast Guard cadet just returned from a successful mission. (Her boyfriend just showed up to bring her lunch.)" Of course, the viewer assumed that the man was in the Coast Guard, and the surprise twist made joining the military sound like a promise to shatter the glass ceiling, erasing the pretty-and-helpless-girl stereotype associated with teenage female identity. In addition to getting

Counter-recruitment poster by Becky Johnson/
SCW, www.syrculturalworks.com

money for college, I wanted to be this strong, independent woman. I was furious that my high school didn't have a Junior ROTC program that would jumpstart my military career.

In the meantime, I packed my schedule full of good classes, played sports after school, and volunteered at a soup kitchen. I took a peer counseling class and I started facilitating domestic violence prevention workshops, feeling stronger as a survivor of abuse. I felt empowered to make change in the world, even if I was only affecting one or two people at a time. The change in my thinking was gradual, of course, but if there is one thing that is sure to deter someone from joining the military, it is feeling confident to reach for your highest dreams without needing the kind of discipline the armed forces offer: harsh orders, violence, and power through physical prowess rather than mediation and dialogue.

When I started my senior year of high school, I decided that even though I grew up in a small town and didn't know what kind of competition I was up against, I would apply to college. If I didn't get in, then I would revisit the option of the military, mostly as a back door into university. I must've applied for dozens of scholarships and to at least fourteen colleges. Filling out the Free Application for Federal Student Aid (FAFSA) form was challenging, particularly because I had no contact with my father and could not supply his information. But with a little help, I finished it and sent it in. Finally, that spring my efforts were rewarded when I received some merit-based scholarships and a large financial aid package based on my financial need to attend Barnard College, an all-women's school in New York City, my dream destination.

While I was in college, I continued to apply for scholarships and aid money. I worked in the financial aid office—a great way to get to know the people who made key decisions about my financial aid package. I applied for loans and grants and kept on working. Throughout college, as I learned more about the way that the United States has repeatedly invaded other countries using military force in the name of democracy and freedom, joining the military began to look less valiant and honorable. In the wake of 9/11, as I watched my brothers and sisters deployed to fight in Afghanistan for what I believed to be an immature and retaliatory response to terrorism, I was relieved that I had not chosen the military path. I became more ardently dedicated toward working for peace, the kind of peace that doesn't come to us via gunpoint or large sums of money. I now work full-time for an organization—Code Pink: Women for Peace—that seeks to end the war in Iraq and bring the troops home now.

I am not writing this down as a "chicken soup for the soul" kind of success story. What I want to highlight is that I did not join the Army because I realized that I had choices and that joining the military was not the only way to go to college or become a strong woman. And at that time, I didn't even know that, according to the Central Committee for Conscientious Objectors, 60 percent of all recruits never receive any money for college.

I meet people my age all the time these days who, after seriously considering joining the military, are making other decisions, which often involve working for social change in their communities. And if I had joined the Army, I may not be alive today to do the peace work that I am doing and to celebrate the world that we are working so hard to save.

Many people are deciding not to join the military, especially for some of the excellent reasons listed in this book. It's a matter of seeing beyond the hype. The military is promising the American Dream: money, college education, travel, adventure, the good life, security and discipline, fraternity and membership into an exclusive group. But, they are delivering a nightmare: death, loss of limbs, broken minds and bodies. Recognizing the flip side of the military coin is the first step; finding other ways to pursue the good life is the natural second.

In our society, an education is a ticket to a stable and sustainable career. Given the state of the economy at the moment, it is unsurprising that 33 percent of male recruits and 39 percent of female recruits report that they enter the military to get money for college.[1] Unfortunately, the military is

---

1. Cohen, William. *Annual Report to the President and the Congress*. Washington, D.C., 2000.

often so desperate to meet quotas and is itself so strapped for cash that these are empty promises; most recruits never see any of this money. Rather than take a gamble on a lot of hot air from military recruiters, it's possible to find tuition money from a reputable source. According to Paul Wrubel, founder of the College Company in San Mateo, California, a cumulative $102 billion is available annually in federal financial aid money alone. Students who qualify are eligible for loans from the federal government, like subsidized and unsubsidized Stafford loans, as well as Perkins loans. (Unfortunately, the Bush administration and Republican-controlled Congress have cut some student aid programs.)

Although little federal funding goes unclaimed, often youth miss out on thousands of dollars in private scholarships simply because they are not aware of them. It doesn't take an honor student or a top-notch athlete to receive these scholarships; many are need-based or just require a bit of focus when thinking about academic goals.

The military advertises job-training programs with instruction in the latest technology, but the truth is that many of the skills Army personnel learn are not applicable in civilian life. More and more people are seeing that military skills are a niche that doesn't really have much of a market, so they are wisely opting for job apprenticeship programs instead. After all, Hummer repair might cull a few job offers outside the military, but general metalworking skills will beef up a resume far more effectively. Often, financial aid is available for training when the field of interest is in high demand. "Many young people are opting to go to trade schools to become skilled in computer science, collision repair, or other labor jobs instead of fighting in this war," said Jackie Alvarez, a program officer at Homies Unidos, a Los Angeles–based organization that works to counter gang violence.

For some, the military promises direction. After high school, it is often difficult to decide on a career path, and this can be frightening for young graduates. But hardly any of the twenty-somethings these days have found their life's calling, even after college. Sometimes a good education, coupled with the simple act of getting one's feet wet in a different job, can be the best tool in deciding on a vocation. When Aimee Allison, a conscientious objector from the Gulf War and a GI Rights counselor (and author of chapter 7), is asked about what to say to youth who are uneasy about their futures and eager to join the military, she advises: "What's the rush? The military will be there in a month or two. But let's consider all the ways you can realize your dreams." Once we take the pressure off and open up the conversation about other possibilities, Allison explained, "young people feel more hopeful about their future and the military doesn't look all that good." After a grueling four years in high school, many young people are understandably not eager to attend college, but this doesn't mean they have to hop into the military in lieu of finding a "real job." Some spend time working or earning money through traveling. Programs such as the Americorps Education Award allow youth to serve around the country and earn up to $4,725 for college money for a full year of service. Another project of Americorps, City Year, encourages youth from ages seventeen to twenty-four to serve in communities to build networks locally and globally. In addition, there are many international organizations that offer subsidized internships, such as teaching English in Japan or volunteering to work with AIDS patients in Africa. Although these programs may not offer money for college, they provide youth the opportunity to travel and be immersed in different cultures—some of the best stuff a fulfilling life, and a good resume, has to offer.

There is a great sense of pride in American culture about serving our country through the armed services—or at least there's a lot of media hype and seductive advertising about it. Though not as visibly glamorous, it takes more honor and courage to dedicate one's life to working for social change. Teachers, community organizers, activists, engineers, public defense attorneys, lobbyists, and artists are the true patriots, the ones who are working to make their country better by countering societal woes—war, poverty, hunger, sickness, and neighborhood violence, to name a few.

Young folks who grow up in low-income areas or troubled households might be attracted to the discipline and strength promised by the military, as a direct contrast to the disorder and loss of control they feel at home. Additionally, the institutionalized violence that the military represents seems to provide a socially acceptable use of street survival skills that might otherwise land a person in jail. When a young person is failing out of school, taking drugs, or experiencing family violence at home, he or she likely feels weak.

"The offer of physical prowess and the power commanded by wearing the Army uniform can become very enticing, beyond the financial incentives offered by the military," suggests Galen Petersen, musician and co-founder of Art in Action, an arts and activism summer camp for underprivileged youth. "But young people are finding these same three qualities—discipline, respect, and strength—through art. . . . In order to put out an effective product, like a CD, a break-dance routine, or a mural, you need to be focused and disciplined. And when you have something to offer to people in your community, you gain respect."

Galen works with youth interested in rapping their stories and making music in Oakland, California. He tells the young people he works with that real strength comes from believing in your own voice and what you have to say. After all, it takes a lot of strength to keep on making art in the face of people who say that you'll never succeed and that it's not good enough. Galen echoed this sentiment when he said, "You have to be strong to not cower in fear of being rejected, to speak your truth."

Adonis (A-1) Walker is one such young person who is resisting the military by creating art. "I'm not going to join the Army," he told me after his solo hip-hop performance at a recent conference about the environment and war. "I mean, there's a war in our neighborhoods that we have to fight before we fight elsewhere. Music is my alternative; I want the world to hear me and what I have to say."

Adonis is a bright, resilient seventeen-year-old with a great sense of humor and a gunshot scar. "Killing doesn't get you anywhere [and] going to the Army is not going to solve anyone's problems," he said. "Get your GED and go to a community college. You don't have to put your life in danger to get an education."

Each of us has choices about what to eat, who to love, who to befriend, who to admire, which sports to play, and which electives to take in school. Ultimately you are the only person who controls your future, even when parents, teachers, government, the cops, and military recruiters tell you otherwise. And you have choices.

I think of all the birthday parties, the report cards, the hot lunches, the dirty socks, the packages of Band-Aids, the haircuts, the crushes, and all the firsts—first dance, first home run, first love, first roller coaster ride—that go into growing a life. Lately, every time I hear about another death in Iraq, all these images flash in my mind. They inevitably end in the same question Cindy Sheehan is asking President Bush, "For what noble cause?"

As I finish writing this chapter, another soldier has just died. His name is John R. Stalvey, a Marine from Conroe, Texas. He was twenty-two years old. For all those that have died so young, I think of how they will never have another memory—not another birthday, not another smile, not another kiss, not another chance. Everything becomes the last.

I am twenty-three, just one year older than John

R. Stalvey was when his life ended. I am scattering these stories about real alternatives into a society that feeds youth guns, TV, cheap fast food, and even cheaper education. I am planting seeds of hope in terrain that has been declared unfit for the cultivation of peace. Maybe a sentence or two of this writing will fertilize a blossoming mind and sprout the idea that when there is no way out, it is not the time to give in to this child-killing machine called the military; it's time to resist.

Resource Guide

College Funding: Scholarships, Grants, and Loans

FAFSA
www.fafsa.ed.gov

Fastweb Search
www.fastweb.com

College Board Search
http://apps.collegeboard.com/cbsearch_ss/
welcome.jsp

Loan Finder
http://apps.estudentloan.com/exec/loanfinder

The Student Guide to Financial Aid (updated each

year) available free by calling (800) 433-3243 or at www.studentaid.ed.gov

Other good college information and financial aid Web sites:
www.freescholarshipguide.com,
www.icanaffordcollege.com,
www.collegeispossible.org,
www.college411.org

If you don't have a U.S. Green Card you can still go to college without paying a fortune. For more information, find organizations, such as the Mexican American Legal Defense and Educational Fund (www.maldef.org), in your area that support immigrant rights and check with your state's public college system to find out if you can pay in-state tuition.

Job Training
Apprenticeships
www.careervoyages.gov

Job Corps
www.jobcorps.org

Americorps, VISTA, and the National Civilian Community Corps hire tens of thousands of people a year to do important, interesting work while earning money for college. For information contact the Corporation for National Service at (800) 942-2677 or www.national service.org.

America's Career InfoNet, an online library for job assistance: www.acinet.org

Traveling and Adventure
Americorps and VISTA (see above)
www.americorps.gov

Outward Bound
www.outwardbound.org

City Year
www.cityyear.org

YouthBuild
www.youthbuild.org

Help rebuild New Orleans
www.commongroundrelief.org

Student Conservation Association
www.thesca.org/cc_bene.cfm

Travel Opportunities
www.idealist.org/career/travel.html

Internships Abroad
www.Internabroad.com

Work or volunteer in England, Ireland, Costa Rica, Ghana, Australia, South Africa, Peru, and more through Bunac Working Adventures Worldwide
www.bunac.org

Art and Activism
Art in Action youth summer camp
www.yesworld.org/events/art.

Activist jobs, internships, and volunteer opportunities
www.idealist.org

Many local organizations and community networks have youth guides to non-military futures that specifically list the resources available in a particular city or state. Contact local peace groups to find out if such a resource exists in your area. Many cities have local youth employment programs, such as American Youthworks (www.ail.org) in Austin, Texas.

Resources for Soldiers, Veterans, and Their Families

Center on Conscience and War
www.nisbco.org

Central Committee for Conscientious Objectors
www.objector.org

Citizen Soldier
www.citizen-soldier.org

GI Rights Hotline
www.girights.objector.org

Gold Star Families for Peace
www.gsfp.org

Iraq Veterans Against the War
www.ivaw.net

Military Families Speak Out
www.mfso.org

Military Law Task Force
www.nlg.org/mltf

Peace-Out
www.peace-out.com

Veterans for Peace
www.veteransforpeace.org

Resources on Civilian Casualties and War Crimes

Amnesty International USA
www.amnestyusa.org

Human Rights Watch
www.hrw.org

Iraq Body Count
www.iraqbodycount.org

Voices in the Wilderness
www.vitw.org

Resources on Peace Groups and Counter-Recruitment

American Friends Service Committee
www.afsc.org

Bring Them Home Now
www.bringthemhomenow.org

Campus Anti-War Network
www.campusantiwar.net

Coalition Against Militarism in Schools
www.militaryfreeschools.org

Code Pink: Women for Peace
www.codepinkalert.org

Committee Opposed to Militarism and the Draft
www.comdsd.org

News on the Growing Counter Military Recruiting Movement
www.CounterRecruiter.net

International ANSWER
www.internationalanswer.org

Iraq Pledge of Resistance
www.iraqpledge.org

Leave My Child Alone
www.leavemychildalone.org

Mothers Against the Draft
www.mothersagainstthedraft.org

New York Civil Liberties Union
www.milrec.nyclu.org

Not in Our Name
www.notinourname.net

Not Your Soldier Youth Counter—Recruitment
Training Camps
www.notyoursoldier.org

Peace Action
www.peace-action.org

Project YANO—The Project on Youth and
Non-Military Opportunities
www.projectyano.org

Purple Hearts
www.purpleheartsbook.com

Syracuse Cultural Workers: Tools for Change
www.syrculturalworkers.com

United for Peace and Justice
www.unitedforpeace.org

War Resisters League
www.warresisters.org